ARRIVAL PRESS

HOME COUNTIES

POETS

Edited

By

SUZY GOODALL

First published in Great Britain in 1995 by
ARRIVAL PRESS
1 - 2 Wainman Road, Woodston,
Peterborough, PE2 7BU

HB ISBN 1 85786 301 1
SB ISBN 1 85786 306 2

Foreword

Home Counties Poets is a collection of verse that gives an insight into how local writers feel about the area in which they live. Among poems about the landscape and nature, nestle works about individuals, the community and their way of life.

I am sure that you will enjoy reading *Home Counties Poets*, and savour this poetic tour guide in the comfort of your own armchair.

Suzy Goodall
Editor

CONTENTS

PROGRESS

When you come to Epsom
Don't drive through the town
As it really isn't fit
For any motorist now.

There are barriers and bollards
And traffic lights galore
There's a very strange diversion
Where the road was straight before.

No one can drive in the town
And no one can drive out
Without enduring long delays
Where there was once a roundabout.

The roundabout has disappeared
And upon the road instead
There is now a Chinese puzzle
Which fills motorists with dread

Once it was plain sailing
Now it causes stress
Is this really progress
Or a bureaucratic mess?

Fire engines with their sirens
Police with flashing lights
Expect motorists to disappear
When there's no space in sight.

It doesn't work, it never will
The motorists all complain
But who will have the courage
To rebuild the old road again?

Mary Rutley

THE WALL

From my window I see a wall
One foot thick and ten feet tall
Built from solid brick and flint
Holding warmth of sunshine's glint.

How was it built? I seem to see -
Work-worn labourer bent at knee,
Calloused hands from daily toil
Lifting flints from Chiltern soil

Where it stands, once was a farm
Was the wall to outlaw harm
Did it enclose a garden fair
Planted by loving hands with care?

Moss and ivy deck the wall
Caress its face and reach up tall
A sparrow pecks the cracks to seek
An insect breakfast with its beak.

Another wall will soon be built
Perhaps with love, perhaps with guilt
Flowers I'll plant beneath this wall
To bring forth love to share with all

Let's strive beyond the walls to see
Life's wonders there for you and me
In every wall there is a door
So open it and seek no more.

Irma Dolphin

GUILDFORD CATHEDRAL

Grandly standing on the hill
Untouched, holy, by its will
Imagine tales of long ago
Like secrets we will never know
Devoted love, pride and care
Forever, always being there
Out of my window, late each night
Rest my eyes upon the sight
Directly at the Cathedral.

Cathedral standing tall and proud
Angel peeking next to cloud
Towering high, strong and fine
Holy aura, worship, shrine
Everlasting dignity
Droves of people come to see
Resting still while time goes by
Angels light against the sky
Long live the Cathedral.

Laura Sharman

TO CROYDON

Croydon is special, Croydon is great
Croydon is friendly just like a mate
Croydon has history, a heart and a past
The years have seen changes the best of them last
Visit our market for bargains galore
See our new library and take time to explore
Our colourful gardens and lovely parks too
All beautifully tended for me and for you
Croydon is magic, Croydon is great.

Anne Campany

SLEEPY RIVER

River, flow slowly, catch all the light
The sun and the moon throw in so bright.
Mirror the boats and mirror the shore,
Mirror my soul, let me think once more.

As swans ride your waters up and down,
Life makes me laugh, then makes me frown.
Boats and their crew chug from lock to lock
As moorhens zig zag from flock to flock.

Ducks treading water to lift in flight
Return to their flock splashing with might.
All friends wanting no more than a swim,
Get fun and games and a choking spin.

Skippers touch caps and wave with their hands,
Distance makes strangers look to be friends.
And as I walk and ponder in vain,
How did I lose out, am I to blame?

River flow slowly, autumn is here,
The one I love is no longer near,
And should you wonder why I do not cry,
I saw the sun dancing in the sky.

Trudi Hoben

SUTTON . . . TO ME

The parks are all gone
The children are bored
They drive their mums mad
At home indoors

Fallen trees and closed down places
Boarded up shops
Boarded up houses
Frowns are what you see
On everyone's faces

Why don't they leave it
And just let it be
So our children can play
And we can all see
Sutton's old history
Like it used to be
And stop building things
We don't really need.

Louise Tippins

LATE FOR SCHOOL

Getting up late is the worst
It means you are going to be last,
Not first
To reach the gate
To stand in line
To get to school well before nine
To beat your friends to the classroom
To be called out in register
So that your teacher doesn't assume
That you are late once again.

Hannah Holland (10)

CROYDON NIGHTS

Mis-matched buildings
Concrete lego land
Mist filled streets
Shopping stands
People like ants
Moving to and fro
Finding somewhere to eat,
Somewhere to go?
Windswept roads
Wet window panes
In Croydon at night
It always rains.

Ian Clack

THE COUNTY'S CHANGING FACE

Drifting scents of summer, and the pigeon's cooing call,
Stubble in the hayfield long ago,
Hauntingly remind me, now that leaves begin to fall,
Of that half-forgotten, ever-present woe.

The thudding of the baler in the golden afternoon
Is background to the tractor's distant roar
And haytime stretches on until we see the harvest moon;
This country child has never wanted more.

The country woman grown now bends her reminiscent gaze
On buildings in the hayfields of before
While monstrous birds of latter days trace the skies with silver haze
And city knocks betimes at country's door.

Sandra Freeman

LOVE

How we love to hear the birds
Sing in the early morn,
See the flowers in the spring
And poppies in the corn.

We love a quiet country ride
Through winding leafy lanes,
With a stop for tea along the way
And home before it rains.

A deep emotion that is felt
Much more than any other,
Is the love a man has for his wife,
A child has for its mother.

It's strange how often we can hurt
Our loved ones with a word.
Make time to talk together, and
Put right what has occurred.

There's nothing so perennial
As a love that you can share,
And we can do so much ourselves
To show loved ones we care.

Phyllis Iden

HAT EYE VIEW

In depths of vision
as clear as most
I stoop to find
then lay my ghost.

And as we strolled
my Joey and I
along our street
now lost in pride.

We both looked up
To the tallow sky
and drank a draught
my Joey and I.

Then we could hear
the hoof and turf
the cold hot oil
the hot cold pies.

And it was clear
so clear he cried
why things do change
why people sigh.

And so we tucked
our mittens deep
slowly nodding
in disbelief.

But he just smiled
to the hollow shops
and tipped my Joey
at passing eyes.

F J Shadwell

A VIEW OF HASLEMERE

I live in a road high on a hill
In a third floor flat even higher still
Many and varied are the sights all around
Making up this small Surrey town
Railway station and churches times three
Swimming pool, car parks, pubs and factories

I live in a road high on a hill
From my flat I look down on trees and rooftops
Watching keen gardeners tending their crops
Some planting flowers and some cutting grass
And when the weather is kind people sit in the sun
Joined by friends at sunset to eat supper outside

I live in a road high on a hill
Tall hedges hide houses away from the fray
Whilst trains at the station rush commuters away
National Trust land surrounds the whole area
With motor-ways, seaside, stately home grounds
All being near and easily found

When the season is right in the distance I see
Outside our Co-op a lit up Christmas tree
A local car park becomes a fairground
Coconuts, dodgems and merry-go-rounds
Also nearby stands a popular pub
Live shows are noisy but with plenty of grub

All these sights help make up this small town
Which I see from the road set high on a hill
In my third floor flat even higher still

Wendy Spence

OUR VILLAGE

How would they have remembered -
Those young men who never returned?
What images of our village would they have taken with them
Those young men who earned
Our eternal gratitude and who we shall never forget?

Did they see
The pure, sparkling waters of the Pang as it gently cleansed
The watercress beds
Not the sluggish stream that must now be artificially cleaned
The frolicking lambs in the meadows gay with ragged robin,
Orchid, cowslip, willowherb and arrowhead
Not the set-aside land or the regularly planted fields artificially greened?

Did they remember
The ever changing colour of the fields as each new crop replaced another
The strength and warm coats of the loyal Shire horses
Or, are these my own memories or images selected by unknown forces?

But I am sure they will have remembered
The brilliance of the evening sun as it transformed the last leaves
Left on the trees in autumn
The swathe of blue and the perfume from the bluebell wood
The smell of new mown hay, the rooks and crows with ebony hood.
The smiling greeting, the caring neighbour
The village cricket competition
The joyful voices raised to praise God for his bounteous provision.

How blessed we are
What memories we shall have
Of our village, now.

Janet Hamblin

HERTS' DELIGHT

From Watford to Welwyn, from Royston to Ware,
From big shopping centre to small market square,
With ample provision for business and leisure
And quaint little villages - oh, such a pleasure,
The new and the old seem to blend and to thrive
Just off the M1 and the M25.

From Baldock to Bushey there's lots to be seen:
The annual revels upon Croxley Green,
Rickmansworth, Letchworth, Knebworth and Tring,
Hatfield House, which is fit for a king,
St. Albans' great abbey and Roman remains,
Within easy access by car, bus and trains.

From Hitchin to Hertford there's much more beside.
Such local delights we acknowledge with pride -
The envy of those who abide other parts,
The beauty we treasure right here in our Herts.

Michelle Hussey

CHANGING BERKSHIRE

It's nice to feel the countryside air,
life without it, what a scare,
The scenery's changed, from green to brown,
The wood and forests, are what they've pulled down,
Think of the wildlife, with nowhere to go,
The builders, they've got no feelings to show,
more and more houses, is what they will build,
and the countryside, it will all be filled.

Julie Titchener (13)

MY HOME TOWN

I am but nine,
but since I've been born
I've lived in East Croydon,
it's not bad at all.

There are things that concern me,
like the cars and their noise.
But I hear there's a remedy,
Tram-link of course.

There's room for improvements,
like more flowers and trees.
But still it's quite pretty,
I hope you'll agree.

The buildings they differ,
Some big and some small.
Some reach to the skyline,
that make me feel small.

And if you look closely,
by day and by night.
You'll see their shapes change,
due to the light.

It's as big as a city,
and one day it may be.
Each year it keeps growing,
Please visit and see.

Emma Bennett

AMERSHAM ON THE HILL

Local shops scattered all around
Families run full of fun
A school girls dream
A happy theme
Of everyone working as a team
That's Amersham my town!

I remember when just a child
A shop called Brownings
Would drive me wild
For his shop was history itself
An exciting adventure, a useful stop

For Mr Browning would excel
Far beyond a shop you know
For as you gazed around
You just did not know what
He would bestow,
From gifts, to wrapping paper
A cup or two and some other things
Which were just too good to be true.

So this is my story
And this is my tale
I just don't know how I could fail
To attract you to such a place,
But I'm afraid it's now changed face!
And Budgens lies in its place.

Nicola Glover-Wright

SORRY SURREY

Surrey's very pretty as I'm sure you'll all agree
Vast with tree framed vistas and historic sites to see
From Runnymede to Box Hill though nothing by the sea.
But its charm is superficial for it's lost identity.

Location is its downfall and is a modern curse
In the past it was a virtue but things are getting worse
For those who work in London it is an ideal berth
The leafy lanes and hidden nooks make heaven upon earth

For everything we pay a price, never clearly stated.
In Surrey's case the cost is high. The people have been fated
In catering for the newcomers to have many homes created
Together with a road network until the county's sated.

Apart from flattened countryside there's another price to pay.
The original population is effectively kept at bay.
Nearly everyone encountered hails from far away
Although living in the South for now they don't intend to stay

Thus society mirrors nature and becomes superficial.
Neighbours aren't a life-long end for they will soon be fickle
And leave for somewhere better in a steady regular trickle
The consequence for Surrey is a nightmare. That's official.

Rowena Shepherd

SUTTON

I've lived in Sutton 30 years,
Had many a laugh and a few tears.

We are lucky to live in a nice place,
Though the 217 is often used for a race.

We've bottle banks and paper banks
and banks for old rags too.
But when we go to the money bank
we have to join a queue.

The St Nicoles centre is very nice.
I have walked around it once or twice.
There are lots of shops empty and to let.
The rent for one is high I bet.

Sutton is not such a pain.
With not much snow, but plenty of rain.

We've lots of parks and open spaces.
And we are just down the road
from Epsom races.

Though the day may be bright of grey.
Sutton is the place to stay.

J M Davidson

DELIGHTS OF SURREY

The countryside of Surrey is beautiful and rare,
And often you see ramblers who pause a while to stare
The river boats and quaint old inns draw people from afar
Which makes a pleasant contrast to driving in a car.
There are pleasure parks, and many, where children love to be,
And sometimes where permitted, you can take a picnic tea.
Once a year at Epsom Downs you can see the Derby run;
Some people travel many miles to join in all the fun.
If you wish to leave the rustic scene and take a trip to town
There are places you can visit that are known to be renown.
After you have made such trips around this county fair
It is likely you will want to make a further journey there.

Sylvia Hills

A SURREY SUNSET SYMPHONY

The sunset has no voice
As it moves across the sky,
Only a golden eloquence
A silent harmony.

No music fills the west
Serenading beauty,
But magic fingers touching heav'n
In unheard melody.

No songs of evening rise
Bidding the day good-bye,
Only a soaring cloud chorale
A wordless rhapsody.

From palest sheen to flame
Creation's artistry
Tunes, as an orchestra to play
The sunset symphony.

J Baker

HERTFORDSHIRE HEDGEROWS

My motor car hummed - a marvellous runner! -
As I sped through the lanes of a Hertfordshire summer;
Open-top freedom was flailing my hair
And threshing my senses, dispensing with care;
The road all awash with shimmering light,
Entrancing my heart and making it bright;
Hedgerows and shadows and berries and bark
Flashed on right past me, but hit on the mark;
By dint of a twist, or a flick of the gear,
My blood would rush faster and throb in my ear,
And the sight of the sunshine and rippling leaves
Gave strength to my feelings and lent my mind ease,
For it binds me to England in such a way
That is ever eternally holding its sway,
High up above me, holding me fast
To a picture of beauty, always to last;
Trunks are the pillars and boughs form the vault
Of a brown-green cathedral composed without fault,
Glowing in glorious pulses and streams,
Flooding my consciousness, filling my dreams
With all that is perfect and pretty and true,
Enabling my spirit to be born anew!

George W MacMahon

CROYDON

Having been a resident of Croydon for 60 years
I could write a book about it, with smiles and some tears
Croydon has changed much, and become a trend setter
But sadly not always changed for the better
In my memory the war years are highlighted
People were then friendlier and more united
I have fond reminiscences of those far off days
With so many attractions that today would amaze
There were pony rides for kiddies in Kennards Arcade
And a hugh alligator in a glass tank laid
Even one day Zulu Warriors were there to thrill
I was a child at the time, and the fright made me ill
On Crown Hill an organ grinder with lively monkey gave pleasure
While in the market one could buy sarsaparilla cheaply for a
generous measure
Entertainment was wonderful, as many cinemas and halls abounded
But perhaps best of all, the Davis Theatre really astounded
With its vast stage to accommodate opera and ballet
Sadly demolished in 1959, and just a plaque on the wall today
The Grand Theatre, where I saw the famous Tod Slaughter play
And the Empire Music Hall, where Max Miller appeared in his hey-day
Coleridge Taylor the composer is a famous Croydon name
Also Peggy Ashcroft the actress, our Grand Dame
Hippodrome Theatre, Pembroke Theatre in The Round, and
Madame Crooks Furniture Store
Wilsons Coffee House, Sanders Bros. Percy and Pitmans - all no more.
Today we do have the Fairfield Halls with its many delights
And the amazing Whitgift Shopping Centre to which shopping invites
Although it is sad we have lost many fine places
In 1995 we are proud of our beautiful parks and open spaces
Many people may talk of Croydon with a frown
But really it's not such a bad town.

Roy Harris

LOOKING AT CROYDON FROM BROMLEY

Oh to be in Croydon
Where the office blocks grow so tall!
Bromley is often called *Croydonised*
But it doesn't compare at all.
Croydon is a vibrant town,
It fairly hums with life.
Walking through its busy streets
You pass the world and his wife.
New shops, new station, new law courts
And the Whitgift Centre renovated,
Croydon's rejuvenation
Is all to be congratulated.
Croydon is the jewel
In outer London's crown.
Bromley may be *clean and green*
But Croydon's a real live town.

Frances Hollingsworth

ESCAPE

From Woking's busy, bustling town
It isn't far to go
To reach the quiet countryside
And nature's finest show.

Small country lanes, with trees galore
And fields where rabbits play,
A multitude of sights and sounds
To while away the day.

How needful is this peaceful time
In days of stress galore -
To wander round the Surrey downs,
You couldn't wish for more.

Margaret Hollis

AS SEEN BY THE EYE OF A BIRD

If you were a bird, your eyes would have seen,
Way down below Surrey is predominantly green,
If I were a bird my nostrils would tell,
The difference 'tween London and Surrey by its smell,
There are miles and miles of unspoilt land,
Not *yet* in the grasp of the developers hand,
The city of London forever extending its creep,
Be careful it doesn't grab you whilst enjoying your sleep,
It's already done it to the lush garden of Kent,
Making damn sure the money's well spent,
A factory here, a car-park there,
They take over the land square by square,
Now is the time to unite hand in hand,
Don't let them take over *our* green and pleasant land!

John Mumford

SURREY'S GLORIOUS GARDENS

Swags of ripe roses, singing with scent,
Frothing over windowsills 'til summer's spent.
Half-timbered houses avalanched by bloom,
Mansions at ease in a flower-filled room.
Bargate stone veined with ivy bound by rue
Petticoats of clematis necklaced through.
Headstrong honeysuckle, ambitious for height,
Fighting with wisteria, wild with delight.
Hollyhocks and lupins, phlox and sweet-pea,
Poppies in profusion, foxgloves marching free.
Marigolds in mayhem, jasmine round the door,
Blue sky for a ceiling, green grass for a floor.
A colourful palette in the open air
Will make a picture beyond compare.

M Foster Hughes

HERTFORDSHIRE LAMENT

I remember fields of green
The town was quaint and so serene
Then folk moved in and changed it all
Buildings that were often tall.
Trees cut down to make more space
Wildlife lost their favourite place.
Motor-ways then marred the scene
New roads criss-crossed the rural green.
Shopping malls and parking space
All to tempt the human race.
Zebra crossings, roundabout
Traffic lights, signs *in* and *out.*
Cars, and yet more on the roads
Lorries with their heavy loads,
The character's completely gone
Few quiet fields to gaze upon.
Where is originality?
Why the change to town and city?
It's a pity and a shame
That soon they'll all look just the same.

Sheila Phelan

HATFIELD SOLITAIRE SURVIVES

Many come because they are lonely,
Others come because they are sad;
Maybe some of them are single,
Perhaps some a mum or dad.

A few just need similar company,
Most enjoy music, dancing, the bar;
Without doubt they all will agree -
Solitaire attracts those near and far.

P V Robbie

PAVEMENTS

The pavements are far too small,
In this lovely place called Ewell,
No people walking side by side,
Single file, you must abide.

A hurdle it is when out in the street,
The old people tut as you meet,
Us younger folk should walk in the road
With pram and kids, so I've been told.

Outside our house no pavement at all,
On the bend is the famous Bourne Hall,
The speed on this road is very high,
Why such speed? Someone will die.

I must cross this road to go to school,
With four small children it's a feat to beat all.
People do say well you shouldn't live there
To be perfectly honest we just weren't aware.

Apart from this problem it's a lovely place,
With lots of greenery and loads of space.
The people are friendly and always polite.
As long as you walk in the road or breathe in tight.

Trudy A Carpenter

LIFE IN CROYDON

Croydon offers many pleasures
Strolls in parks, in woods, on commons
Walking in modern shopping precincts
Browsing round large stores at leisure.

A large new library caters for all
Providing books on every subject.
Fairfield Halls presents variety
With entertainment in every aspect.

Neither is Croydon's past forgotten
Historic memories still remain
In monuments, the almshouses, the Old Palace,
Where archbishops dwelt for centuries,
Its ancient interior just the same
With old oak timbers, creaking floorboards
All preserved within its frame.

Surrey Street, site of market traders,
Is highly resistant to all invaders
Its cobbled street withstanding time:
Even capturing royalty
Marvelling at its longevity.

So life in Croydon
Can give enjoyment
To those who seek
The most fulfilment.

Barbara Carpenter

THE RIVER MOLE
NEAR BOX HILL, IN SURREY

Across a fallow field and over a river
whose waters are now once more in spate.
A chalky, muddy and murky state.
Winter rain from Downland Hill chalk.
A river which in a dry season
can be little more than a Downland Chalk stream.

On its far bank a gently rising grass slope,
sparsely wooded with beech, box and oak.
Along its high ridge an unkempt hedge
and here winds the pilgrims path,
trod over the years by many feet.

Through this Downland of chalk and flint,
a river named Mole, flows.
A river which as it crosses a flat plain
near the great hill called Box, has in its bed holes.

A shy river that in summer often hides below ground,
becomes in a season of heavy rain a plunderer of the surrounding plain.
A sound and peaceful sleeper who walks in a disturbed sleep.

The cause, a dream perhaps of long long ago, when all
this chalk was an ocean floor and this plain its shore.

Peter Young

CROYDON

I sit by my window
and what do I see
The cars on the fly-over
racing past me
Life in Croydon
goes so fast
Let's sit down for a while
and remember the past.

When I was a girl
we played in the park
It never mattered if
you stayed out till dark
Leave your door open
come in for a tea
My neighbours and friends
all welcomed me.

Now all you see
are offices and flats
People too busy to
stop for a chat
We've got Tescos and Sainsbury
and superstores to see
All tempting you with offers
of buy one get one free.

So come on Croydon
what can you do
To make life more pleasant
for me and for you.

J M Jennings

ON MY CLOUD

I've seen the war planes come and go.
Watched the sky line grow and grow.
The gentry's houses stood so proud.
All disappeared beneath the clouds.
I remember well the old town hall
In all of Croydon stood so tall.
Saturday cinema was such fun
To watch the film then home to mum,
Sunday morning in Wandle Park
Where all the dogs would run and bark.
The kids would sail their boats and such
Fishing for tadpoles but not catching much.
But now it's such a busy place
I scarcely know anyone's face.
The market street I must admit
Is just the same where I used to sit.
And so I join the busy crowd
Still living here up on *my cloud.*

Emma Dymond

TIMES PAST

We loved that hill, so long ago
Under the bridge I think of still
We loved and laughed, and sometimes cried.
Pressed lips so hard, with passion sighed.
What memories, what treasured hours,
Those golden times, that all are ours.

Dee Largent

CROYDON: PRIDE V PREJUDICE

This is to all those who run Croydon down:
We're bravely admitting *we're proud of our town!*
You can keep your Dulwich and brash Crystal Palace:
We've got it *all* in our glass *petit-Dallas.*

The Whitgift, of course, is a shopper's delight,
We've the liveliest of discos, for souls of the night!
We're artistic people, so when culture calls,
We all rush on down to our great Fairfield Halls.

To Surrey Street market we all often scoot,
For quality and cheapness of fresh veg. and fruit.
If world-wide cuisine is your *cup of tea,*
A wider selection there just could not be.

Metrobus *hoppers* are really a boon,
And East Croydon Station was made on the moon!
We're handy for London *and* Sunny-South-Coasting . . .
Our future tram system deserves champagne-toasting!

Outside the centre, we've villages like Shirley,
Addiscombe, Sanderstead - don't forget Purley -
Our community networks are strongest by far,
Successfully keeping things *just as they are*!

In short, our town's fine points are better than most,
So come on, you locals: *from Croydon*! please *boast!*
And to those *unenlightened* who like to decry it -
All I can say is 'Don't knock, 'til you've tried it!'

Sue Millward

COUNTIED OUT

As London gradually expanded
Into the city we know today
Middlesex county was disbanded
All but the name was thrown away.

Adjoining counties were given orders,
To annex parts within their borders
But to this day the legend persists
That the county still exists.

The Cricket Club proudly bears the name
Such is the MCC's fame.
And the Royal Mail, though very thorough
Has never deserted the borough.

So if you should inadvertently
Address a letter geographically
Don't be surprised if the postman rejects
Your Surrey direction and writes *Middlesex.*

The inhabitants wait to hear
What they'd find welcome tidings:
That Middlesex might one day reappear
Just like Rutland and the Ridings.

Ann Hobbs

A PLEASANT KINGDOM

A pleasant kingdom Surrey was,
Or so it seemed to me,
It used to stretch from London Bridge,
But it never reached the sea.

Over downwash-gravels and London clay,
The little train now speeds its way,
Slows down at Guildford, to *a walk.*
Then onwards through a wall of chalk.

High on the Downs we used to go,
Down from Haslemere,
Where in the forest down below.
We lunched outside at Shere.

All's still there for those that look,
The Downs, the valleys, farms and lanes,
Still here and there an iron-stained brook,
The distant spires with sunlit vanes.

On this kingdom of the hills,
That's leafy Surrey, and on me,
The summer sunlight spills
Here at Chiddingfold . . . at tea,
Quiet here, beside the streams;
Of this, the tired commuter dreams.

F G Gilbert-Bentley

THE LOST WOODLAND TO WINDMILL COMMON

I walked through the woods but the trees were not there
And all around lay flat and bare.
Where are the badgers, the foxes, the deer?
They are gone forever - I fear
Soon there'll be buildings and roadways in place
Of the beautiful woodland once in this space.
Gone are the bats that fly at night
Pretty woodpeckers are now out of sight
Children no more will play on this land
Taken from us by cruel demand
These trees no more will bend and moan
On the soft soil they have been thrown
Tall pines and oaks cut to the ground
No mice or adders to make a sound
In years to come no one will see
Those beautiful trees so dear to me

Mary Loader

BOXHILL

A summers day - the warmth of the sun
A place to sit for everyone
Lovers hold hands and children play
It's a green and wonderful place to stay.
Looking down on the world below
Laid out like a train set from long ago.
'Mummy, look, there's a tiny car!'
Says a child amazed at seeing so far.
Drivers shouldn't stop but they always do
Trying to catch a glimpse of the view.
Ice-creams, sunshine, a smile on a face
God must have been smiling when he made this place.

Barbara Little

CHINTHURST HILL

When all around is calm and still
Nature's breath is on the hill
I crave the wind upon my face
So head straight for my favourite place
Climbing up the zig-zag path
I revel in the aftermath
Of scented pine, from hillside torn
The fragrance strong when newly sawn
This may seem sad but there is good
In making way for native wood
Then to the tower atop the brow
Crudely boarded, crumbling now
Once a person's much loved folly
Obscured in part by yew and holly
I'll sit awhile on fallen tree
Worn smooth by others just like me
Taking in the view beneath
Of Wonersh, Guildford and Blackheath
And when it's time for me to leave
I thank the hill for this reprieve
And warn it I'll be back next week
With kids in tow for hide-and-seek!

Cheryl Foote

THOUGHTS OF CHEAM

The place where one lives and works
Is often taken for granted,
It's easy to see what is wrong
But not the things to advantage.

And yet if one has to leave
It's amazing how much is missed.
A self contained unit itself
Cheam Village contains a long list.

There's ancient and modern adjacent,
A history full of interest,
A large part preserved for our pleasure
Some gone on a whim or behest.

An old timbered farmhouse, Whitehall,
And a cottage from years long past,
A chapel from earliest days,
All cared for that they may last.

To both sides of Cheam, open space.
The largest and best to the west,
A park and gardens for pleasure
A playground for children to test.

Within the park a walled garden
Shut off from the traffic beyond
A place to be quiet and peaceful
Just flowers and occasional birdsong.

Almost the best place by far
In Cheam, is the library near by,
For readers so much to enjoy,
For listeners or viewers, tapes to try.

I'd like to be back in Cheam,
To see once more the tree-lined roads,
To visit again the park so green,
With thoughts of Cheam I pen this ode.

Jeanette Bath

RENOVATION CHAOS IN GUILDFORD

I remember years ago or so it seems to me
When I looked out of the window, a pleasant sight I'd see.
Nice green lawns and shrubs and trees, adding colour to the place,
Shoppers strolling quietly by, contentment on their face.
But now for months and months and months, or so it seems to me
A glance out of the window brings abject misery.
There's piles and piles of flagstones, some broken and awry,
There's wood and cones and rubbish, it's enough to make you cry.
There's pipes and sand and cement and plastic orange net,
Every day more debris and it hasn't ended yet.
The residents are pasty faced, they're lacking good fresh air,
The dust, it gets in everywhere, and the noise is hard to bear.

The lovely beds where grass once grew, well only weeds are seen
I suppose we should be grateful, at least they're fresh and green.
There's great almighty puddles when the rain comes pouring down,
We'll soon be needing dinghies to get us into town.
When it all is finished, it will be great it's said,
Not for the present residents - *We'll probably all be dead.*

Nellie Heard

SURREY

Going home from Waterloo to Surrey
Signifies a world that's in a hurry,
With its trains, its cars and its motorways,
Creating noise that spoils our tranquil days;
And winter's fog and wind and lashing rain
Make us long for warmth and green spring again.
Perhaps we sit at home and watch TV,
Glimpse holidays that take you to the sea.

But the heart of Surrey is a jewel,
Starting maybe from Epsom and from Ewell,
When tardy spring and flowers now arrive,
The Downs turn mild and nature comes alive,
Then is the time to walk down leafy lanes,
To exercise our legs, to disperse pains,
To visit Dorking and nearby Box Hill,
And lovely Mickleham, so quiet and still.

Or maybe you prefer Friday Street or Shere,
For a good day's walk, ending with a beer
At some quiet pub, before you make your way
Back to your home, to end a blissful day.
Of course, there are many other places,
Such as Derby Day at Epsom races
In this dear county, sheltered from extremes,
Where you can choose the spot to dream your dreams.

Or, boating on rivers, fishing in streams,
Visiting churches, admiring oak beams,
Trips to the Oval to watch the cricket,
Seeing batsmen perform at the wicket.

It's all there in this fine county of ours,
Go out and see its magic and powers.

Paul Rowden

WAGGONER'S WELLS

Shimmering like topaz beneath the hills
the jewels of Surrey lie deep and still.
Mirroring oaks and beech trees in sandy dells
casting leaves as coins into wishing wells.
Only the brown backed fish disturb the waters
in rippling circles, as they nose the air,
while dragonflies on brittle wings, skip and skim
each kissing like Narcissus, his own image.

Wild fowl weaving in between the reeds
with honking tones, call broods to heed
where the fishermen are set
with small camp-stools and large keep-nets.
As the artist, humbled, seeks to capture
with his colours and brushes, some of the rapture
that dwells; in this beauty spot
known as Waggoner's Wells.

Catherine Curtis

VALEDICTION

In trepidation we stand in the Sublunar zone
Waiting to rise up to galaxy's unknown
far and wide we will seek
beneath the ocean very deep.
Longing to possess a translunar gift,
maybe of gold or of love.
It cannot be a myth.
Our short trip upon the earth
from the very day of birth,
is compensated for when we pass up above the moon.
The end is so distant from doom.

Natasha Annette Truss

RIP RICKMANSWORTH HIGH STREET?

For those who live in Rickmansworth,
It's easy to complain
About the quietness in town
- lots of people say the same.

Just walk along the High Street,
You'll see it's sometimes bare,
But if the shops were all closed down,
Would many of us really care?

For just towards the outskirts,
A thriving empire grows,
A lure for *Ricky's* residents,
I mean of course - *Tescos!*

And folk that really can't afford,
To pay their weekly bills,
Sunday morning, *car- booting*,
Is guaranteed to cure all ills.

Meanwhile our poor shopkeepers,
They toil to make ends meet,
But rates are high and profits low,
And some of them accept defeat.

So when the shopping comes to mind,
Please try and think ahead,
For otherwise these High Street shops,
May very soon be dead.

Carol Hiscock

THEN AND NOW

Time can be retraced. Barbed wire
Remembered and 'No Access'
To the sea. Squat concrete blocks
Obstructing paddling. Castles
And rounders on the beach - all forbidden.

One remembers sweets rationed to treats
On Saturday. Sirens wailing, planes droning outward
To the sea. Army tanks that lined the streets
And grinning soldiers whistling
At pretty girls - all forbidden.

Sea mists lift, the years have passed.
Alone on shingle now the sands smile
Back. Children laugh, skip, build castles,
Paddle and swim. They are happy; but us?
It is too late - all forbidden.

Esther Weatherill

GO BY SHANKS' PONY

Walk through beechwoods when the bluebell flowers,
Or in winter when frosty days abound.
Shelter there from sudden summer showers,
Listen to the raindrops' pattering sound.
Uplift your spirits if you're feeling down
In Chiltern beechwoods of such sweet renown.

Or by the Thames you may prefer to stroll,
Watching boats and diverting river birds.
Make Bourne End to Marlow town your goal,
Where views defeat, my prosaic words.
Then if you're too weary to amble back,
A train runs along the railway track.

Nancy Wright

MY GUILDFORD

Guildford it a town of noise, pile drivers, pneumatic drills
Screaming sirens ringing tills, demolition crashing, bumping
Amplifiers jiving jumping. Alarms non-stopping through the night
Screeching brakes and motor bikes red eyed monsters petrol burning
At nerves and ear drums churning churning. Refuse eaters wailing moaning
Constant drum of traffic droning. Drowning in a sea of sounds
Torn by metal slavering hounds. There's no respite, no release
But yet . . . Guildford also is a town of peace.

Rolling Downs that meet the blue, brown old river flowing through,
Kingcup fields where gentle cows stand and chew and lie and browse,
Bluebell woods and leafy byways far from crowded noisy highways
Where wild life dares to have no fear, birds, squirrels and fallow deer,
Where jangling nerves and mind relax, away from the
I'm all right blow you Jacks!

In quiet grounds the castle dreams, reflecting mediaeval scenes,
The town clock ticks away the ages, watching Guildford's turning pages.
And on the hill above the town, cathedral's angel gazes down
Upon the pot pourri below, of people people hurrying scurrying
Living, loving, hating, worrying.
So many facets so many ranges, but human nature never changes,
It's *people* through the centuries down
That are the nucleus of Guildford town.

Lorna Butcher

NATURE RESERVE

I stand in the park.
The blustering wind chilling my face.
As thoughts fill my mind
I want to express my happiness,
This beauty, so simple and basic,
Available to all. But do we all see it?
An oasis amid building. A haven of peace,
In spite of the rubbish that's dumped,
And the dogs who defecate.
In spite of the abandoned burnt-out cars
And wrecked motor bikes.
In spite of the empty drink cans
And the paper and plastic blowing about.

I walk in the park.
In spring, this place comes alive.
With a succession of colour, buds open, trees blossom.
Elderberry, sloes and crabapple.
Frothy white cow parsley spreads through the wood
Covering the dead leaves and litter beneath.
Skylarks soar in the sky
Piercing the air with their song.
Magpies meet in a crowd, choosing their mates.
Black crows dance in the grass,
And a thrush builds her nest in a hawthorn.
A kestrel sits on a post, surveying the scene,
As a vole trembles, and runs for his hole.

Pauline Smith

OF BATCHWORTH HEATH

Scruffy scrub, painted pub,
Bumpy ground, trees surround;
Round the side houses hide,
Riders hack muddy track.

Noble arch steals a march,
Moor Park's door, golfers' 'Fore!'
Lofty view . . . Traffic queue,
Many signs, road's white lines.

Cars bustle, vans hustle,
Lorries halt, no one's fault,
Left and right, corners tight,
Traffic's welter . . . Timbered shelter.

Uneasy mix, suburban fix,
London meets country's feet.
Wilderness; weariness;
Battered heath, Batchworth Heath.

Pam Pointer

MIMRAM OLD FRIEND

The water has gone, all gone away,
It rained in August,
Stuck inside too wet to go out and play,
The river is dead,
It was there yesterday,
I used to feed ducks, watch stone loach play,
Sticklebacks, Bullheads, Trout in a stream,
Six weeks in the summer, every boys dream.
The water board charge, we all have to pay,
I wonder if they listen,
Our streams gone away.

Ron Thompson

CROWTHORNE BERKSHIRE 1930'S

A busy little village, more like a town to me
No thatched cottages or front rose gardens there to see.
Unmade roads and avenues with hedges and trees
Behind them hid big houses, the *gentry* lived in these.
Our schooling was adequate, the building very cold
We certainly in those days did as we were told.
Walking to church in line to celebrate a *Saints* day
Dancing round the Maypole, usually a chilly day in May.
My bicycle was my pride and joy, although was never new
I knew where every chestnut tree, primrose and violet grew.
The friendly village shops, Douglas's, The Mart, and Rogers
The bakers to name a few
Not forgetting Macy's and Bells, where the accumulator
was charged when due.
Mr Knight the Chemist had a remedy to put us right
Mr Noakes the Postmaster was always so polite
Though times have changed for Crowthorne, it is
still a welcome sight.

Violet Langton

ST ALBANS

St Albans is a wonderful city,
The park is nice and the lake is pretty,
There's an ancient cathedral, a clock tower too,
And if you get bored, there's plenty to do:
You could go swimming, have a look round a shop,
There's a great big hill, you could climb to the top,
You could eat your lunch in a restaurant,
You could go to the cinema if you want,
Even the Roman's thought it was nice,
When you find St Albans, you find paradise.

Gemma Crisp (12)

RETURNING

Arriving back from grinding city streets
Into the evening warm of river meadows,
I saw through hedges, patient standing sheep
Enjoy the sloping sun in quiet fields,
Their little lambs all still now at their sides,
And noticed blackthorn blossoming nearby,
And hawthorn, green and ready to be picked
By hungry children calling, 'Bread and cheese!'
On reaching home I threw my things aside,
And marched along to check familiar sights,
The forest brow, still wrinkled at the sky,
The bridge still bandaged in intensive care,
The narrow lanes, quite dry and empty now,
The river in a better mood, and almost kind,
Grown thoughtful, contemplating peace at last,
And all the lovely summer yet to come.
I vowed to guard my days and stay at home.

Ann Elliott Wall

DREAMY DAYS

Hills flowing like ripples of sea,
Luscious grass walking with me.
Golf balls flying through the air,
Dogs barking without a care.
Washing drying on the washing line,
People in pubs drinking wine.

In the classrooms we're all working hard,
And children in the kitchen are baking with lard.
There is a clatter,
The milk is late but that does not matter.
Neighbours are happy and smile at me,
Buckinghamshire is a wonderful place come and see!

Rebecca McLaughlin (10)

HOMETOWN

A climb from Rickmansworth via Scots Hill
Leads to the spread of Croxley, our town.
Where once cartwheels rumbled on stony tracks,
Now exhausting engines vie on metalled routes.
As decade turns from decade and changing years go on.
Thoughts dwell on gentler times, alas, forever gone.

The green with the stillness of early morn
Lies tranquil before the onset of bustling day.
Trees in winter dress loom eerily through the mist,
Tell-tale trails in dewy grass criss cross the open space.
Thus can the legend of ghostly coach and pair
Take small imagination to see it gliding there.

With an abundance of inns and churches proud
Well met are the spiritual and social needs.
A library, risen from the ashes of the old,
Is amply stocked within its pleasing walls.
Much is offered in the way of stores,
From lamb chops to drawing pins, the choice is yours.

A fox at the door, and badgers in pairs,
With an occasional deer, sighted at feed.
Colourful woodpeckers swing on the nuts, and,
Many a blackbird tunes up for the dawn.
A sound on the willow as it cracks at the ball;
Each year, the *Revels*, a welcome for all.

Fishermen drowse patiently along the canal
As quiet drifting barges cause the gentlest of waves.
'Neath varied wooded trees meander shady paths,
A horse clops to view and as suddenly is gone.
With such a panoramic passing scene.
Lives are enriched in Croxley Green.

Lizbeth Cooke

MY PLACE

Oh what a joy it is to live in Croxley Green
Between Watford and Rickmansworth is where it can be seen
Lots of people come to visit from near and far
Some by aircraft and train, whilst others use the car

Many have been privileged to write on Croxley Script
A quality writing paper that is very rarely ripped
Once made in a factory by the river Gade
It may have gone now, but the paper certainly stayed

Despite the size of this little piece of land
There are lots of friendly people who would gladly lend a hand
So rest assured and cast away your doubts
The people of Croxley Green are not a bunch of louts

With so many characteristics too numerous to list
Why not! I hear you cry, oh if you insist!
If you visit our new library packed full of books
The design of this alone is sure to get some looks

For those who wish to travel by using the train
There is not one, but two stations to help ease the strain
Whilst wildlife lovers come to visit at our local moor
With its undulating surface, leaves many feeling sore

When summer comes upon us, everyone is keen
To visit all the attractions, including Revels on the Green
With the waiting list for new-comers not about to give
For them it's true that Croxley is, the only place to live

Trevor I Bale

ST ALBANS

Whispering city of flint stone remains
Your crumbling walls resound with the strains
Of Roman existence, echoing still,
As ghostly Centurions march on the hill.
There stands the cathedral, mighty in form
Proclaiming the first Christian martyr to fall,
The shrine of St Alban encased within
A Pilgrim's retreat, embroidered in stone.

Then wandering down to the valley below,
Scenes from a Bruegel landscape show
Watery isles and mirrored trees,
Where glowing children, in twos and threes
Slide prisms of ice on a frozen lake,
Cold glassy clusters which shatter and break,
Scattering fragments away and afar
To distant skies blending into the shore.

And graceful airborne swans make haste
Gliding to find a resting place,
With mallard ducks and geese they weave
To huddle in corners, prepared for the freeze,
As evening mists hold the air with a chill
And lakeside banks grow distant and still.
Another night from another time
Echoing city, tonight you are mine.

L Whitton

URBAN FOX

Have you heard the cry in the night,
The cry of souls in pain?
It travels the roads
Like a floating ghost
Repeating again and again.

One morning it sounded once more,
That plaintive cry I knew
And over the fence
To rest on a shed,
A beautiful vixen flew.

Supple and fleet with luscious fur,
Tipped tail and darked marked paw,
Regarding the gardens;
Outstaring the cats,
Until melting away once more.

At 3 o'clock she barked last night,
I saw her weave our street
And her jaunty step
Was dogged indeed
By the fox who will make her complete.

Margaret Hargrave

WHAT NOW SLOUGH

(A rebuke to Sir John Betjeman)

Come, unfriendly bard - revisit us - revoke your incantation
Repent your tortious toxic fuss - recant your invocation
Hang up your robes, fold your wings, return to us from glory
Shelve your harp, still its strings, to learn the *new* Slough's story
Just let your shade descend to view
Slough's fair, full-grown fulfilment - deride the old admire the new
A happy, hopeful fusion of many nations, colours, creeds
Dovetailed in equality, conscious of each other's needs
United in harmony.
Were you too sober, meek and mild, too frugal, mealy minded
To evaluate Slough's raunchy style - to her punchy virtues blinded?
Slough stimulates, electrifies, is resolute and brisk
Conceived as a terraqueous town now soars with grace to space.
Slough swims in thickly sensuous fumes redolent of Mars
And acrid pungent sickly pongs of bitumen tars
We watch with wonder plumes of spume power packed
Crowning warehouses with products stacked
To save and feed a world in need - our pride our town
our *Slough*

Liz Horder

EPSOM COMMON ON EASTER DAY

(Ode to a sad friend)

Now violet clouds are banking in far sky,
Cold breezes pass the pussywillow by
Rippling brown fern fronds, curled and sere,
To stay the silver birch from leaf, just here.
Whilst up ahead three magpies splash around
In water left by rains on rutted ground.

Aloft in ancient oak the raucous jay
Gives warning call of *stranger on the way!*
Pass by the fallen trunks of once-noble trees . . .
Pass by marsh plants, where drone the honey bees
Into the tangled coppice. Here graceful roe deer
Like silent shadows graze, then, wraithlike, disappear
To distant glades, where velvet mosses green
Lie sudden sun-dappled in iridescent sheen.

Haste now, good friend, to walk alongside me.
The beauty of this heath shall ever be
Safe refuge from man's blind unreason,
For her mantle changes only in due season.

Glenys N Gadd

GROVESIDE CLOSE

'Groveside Close, you sure about that?'
Said the driver of the cab in his brown checked hat
'In the A-Z there seems no such place'
'It's the site of the old laundry' I say with a reddening face
'Next to Muschamp, along from Wrythe Green
It's a new road surely you must have seen . . .'
'Shall I stop for a minute and ask a passer by?'
'*No* just follow *my* directions, please,' I cry
'You sure it's not Grosvenor, there's one nearabouts'
'*I know where I live*,' though I'm now having doubts
'It's not far from here,' spotting a familiar site
Finally seeing an end to my plight
'Oh, the new road, love. Why didn't you tell me?'
'I did,' I mumble while locating my door key
I emerge from the cab, at last on the pavement
While the checked hat driver tots up the fare payment
'£12 from Purley seems expensive,' I say
'Well, that's your fault love, for not knowing the way!'

Debbie Edwards

WANBOROUGH MORNING

Wind blows on the dull day,
as tumbling leaves fall in disarray,
a mantle of damp pervades the scene,
and the lustre is lost to the foliage green.

The shivering day attempts to wake,
but tired mist paints the morn' opaque.
Weary stillness encompasses wide,
pre-autumnal's drear low tide.

Requiem tears, for summer's close,
yet refresh the morning's doze.
Anticipation creeps through the air,
for festive splendour soon to share.

Now familiar kestrel's flight,
hovers high, in cloudless sight.
Shrew, in rigormortis set,
upon the pathway where death was met.

Stagnant stream awaits strong rain,
to fulfil, restore, it's course reclaim
as moat betwixt the path and lines,
three journey-ways, on the same curved vines.

Commuter trains, manic sought,
city turmoil; synthetic bloodsport.
Racing, cutting with sound and track
country calm, time-traced back.

Lines to transport the rested few.
and, the many over anxious, who
are blind to the balm they slice with speeds
rushing to bedlam, as babel recedes.

M Lawrence

BERKSHIRE SPRING

Eyes weep onion tears to flavour winter stew
But through the kitchen window
Spring invades my nostrils
To spin my spirit that is winter bound.

Humble sparrows for the labourer
Chatter in frost bitten brambles
And blackbirds scatter quavers
To hang upon bare branches.

I know that spring has reached her destination
Not by peeping buds or birdsong
But that my quarantined spirit
Has broken its chains to greet her.

Catherine M Hamblin

NATURE'S PROTECTORS

Our Surrey trees spread far and wide,
Oh what tales they could tell,
From Windsor Great Park to the humble Shere woods
At what price would their stories sell?

They stand tall like soldiers around us,
Filtering sunlight or keeping us dry,
They fight the pollution we live with,
Oh you humans! They seem to sigh.

So in the hustle and bustle of Surrey,
Stop, look around and enjoy,
The breath taking beauty of nature,
In our trees we must never destroy.

Valerie Hoare

THE LAND THAT TIME FORGOT

Hustle and bustle, worry and stress,
Scant time for friendships, nor even for rest.
Achieving, commuting, fume laden air,
Life was motorway madness, urban despair.

So, to the Herefordshire borders we came,
Searching for calm and a life that was sane.
And it's here in a place called *the land time forgot*,
That we've found perfect peace in a God-given spot.

The gently rolling countryside soothes the restless eye,
Whilst tranquil brooks and rivers glide effortlessly by.
Quiet, winding lanes criss-cross the land with ease,
Like shining maypole ribbons bending gently in the breeze.

Quaint, historic villages are major players on this stage,
Their cottages of black and white sharing secrets of a bygone age.
And there is always time to stand and talk of this and that,
O'er fence or gate, in lane and street, on lonely hillside track.

Whilst from my cottage windows I can see
A host of wildlife close to me.
Fox cubs and badgers 'round my borders prowl,
And bathed in shimmering moonlight glides the ghostly owl.

The Herefordshire soil is tinged a dusky red,
Made fertile by the blood which many men have shed.
For centuries, brave men have fought and died to own this spot,
And now I see why passions flowed for this, *the land that time forgot.*

Heather Philpott

SUTTON

What a wonderful town is Sutton
Its high street is bright as a button
Its pavements are clean, its grass is so green,
And its butchers sell lamb and not mutton.

There are plenty of jobs all around
Its economy seems to be sound
There are so many shoppers, street singers and boppers
And talent in plenty abounds.

So please folks don't run it down
Be proud of your very own town
The malls are so bright and its stores a delight
A real jewel in the crown.

So when watching the news on TV
And the earthquakes and fighting you see
Just spare a thought on this London *resort*
And the fact that you're happy and free.

M Smith

SPRING

The birds are singing their sweet song,
To let us know Spring won't be long.
The thrush the wren the robin too,
Sing out shrill songs for me and you.
The bulbs are lifting their small heads,
Lifting themselves from their warm beds.
The Winter has been cold and long,
It's lovely to herald the end with a song.
We take the Lord's gifts so lightly,
They cost us not a thing,
A bird a song, a bulb a flower,
Thank God for everything.

P Saunders

SURREY'S LAMENT

As each verdant hill enhances our view,
Surrey tells of its story to me and to you;
One of pilgrims and castles, warriors too.
Footsteps through history.
Marching in time.

Sighing rivers proclaim their melodic tale,
Dancing in sunlight, along each wooded vale;
Patchwork of colour, never ceasing to fail.
Heartland of Surrey.
Beating in time.

Oh, Surrey of mine, will you endure,
The passage of time, now seeking your core?
Bulldozer and landspill, superseding folklore.
Hour-glass of memories.
Time running out.

Christina Faith Tomkins

SWAN LOVE

Sacred is the secret of my Hertfordshire love
Shining beauty escapes within your kind
hazel eyes
The swan-like grace of your elegant figure
Feeling and knowing your love
Warms the chilled and broken cracks within
a wounded heart

Needing you is needing the breath of life
Without you the swan would drown
in her sorrow.

T J Beatty

FLOWERS

Alas! Summer is leaving us now
Sweet flowers are gradually taking their bow,
Dainty lobelias are gracefully fading
Beautiful roses their petals are falling.

How handsome the dahlias are
But soon now they will disappear,
Gladioli and iris the tall flags are sighing
Begonia and hollyhock are sadly withering.

Lily of the valley it fascinates me
Growing under the old laburnum tree,
Margaretta as in a whisper she does sing
If Mother Nature does her job
You'll be here in the spring.

June E Baden

SONNET OF CROYDON

A few pockets remind of yesteryears,
The Whitgift Almshouses, the Old Palace,
And old Surrey Street Market's friendly face.
Conservation sees that less disappears.
Papers tell of crimes that arouse one's fears.
In olden times Middle Row was the place!
A century ago, such a disgrace!
The town's probably no worse than its peers.
Then of course it's not everybody's dish.
They flee by train, bus - perhaps now by tram?
And there are many things can get one down.
The man with his tank - on his roof a fish!
All the litter shows some don't give a damn,
But all in all Croydon's not a bad town.

David South

WINTER MAGIC

Deep midwinter drifts gently into spring.
Brave snowdrops defy the icy winds,
Standing firm against the leaden sky,
And catkins toss in a manic dance
With alder, and yellow aconite . . .
Snowdrops friend waits for winter sunshine
To open its petals for a glimpse
Of hope that the warmer days will bring.

Shapely spreading ash . . . grey olive tinged bark,
Hard black velvety buds, late to leaf.
Frayed leaves and stems, transformed, frosty edged
Into unbelievable beauty.
A fairy world, but of deep blue cold
Beyond all imagination.
A fiery sunset briefly flames,
Then is lost in mist across the park.

Ivy Allpress

HOG'S BACK ON A SPRING DAWNING

Caught by the daylight on a greening slope
Pale flints brood stiffly in their barren scrapes,
Grotesquely dumb, waiting for kind
Concealment in the crop's whispering sea.

Rain eases pain of tightening bark and bud,
Washes stale winter from the thrush's notes,
Attends to billions of unstated needs,
Reshapes the flints by importunity.

And ancient in a dream of roots, earth-sweet,
The Hog becomes the season's monument,
Untroubled by fly-tickling time or men
Walking his flanks in rain.

Michael Tanner

HORSELL COMMON

Brightness tumbles through the branches,
Falling amber, gold and red.
Gilded birch and leather oak leaves:
A dappled bridle-path ahead.

Fungi swell like silent time-bombs,
Hang like roosting bats on trees.
Dog is snuffing scented moistness:
Sagging bracken tugs our knees.

Across the road and through the pine-wood,
Silent needles underfoot,
Branches thick with gloom above us,
Path-way dim and rough with roots.

Springy turf and open vistas:
Clean-washed blue and welcome breeze:
Heather still with tardy blossom
Billows from the shore of trees.

Slow-foot dog lags far behind now,
We stand and wait, solicitous.
The sunset sky a benediction,
Fiery clouds and hint of frost.

Juliette Edwards

DISTANT DAYDREAM

(To Jane)

Nestled there, village in the valley,
Busy, friendly under stormy skies,
Or bursting with new life in spring.

Hedges and hills, whose panting pedestrians
Just smile, enjoying the exercise
As they push prams, the wind in their hair.

Bumpy bus chugs uphill too, giving
A mini-marathon tour of the topography,
Choking around corners, collecting polite passengers.

Cheerful companions at church; familiar faces
Warm and welcoming. Christmas cold
Only cultivates our soaring spirits.

Chasing children clutching their satchels
Stream out of school, while mothers
Stand chatting outside miniature shops.

Dusk, and the dutiful angel smiles on her domestic dominion;
Her panoramic view the pillowed village,
Lighting the lap of green and gold;

A temperate tapestry whose moderate transition
Is just enough for the young,
But not too rushed for the rest.

In my heart I see September days,
Bright and blowy with remnants of a recent summer;
Then sublime sunsets crowning a spellbound gallery.

I still run through your flowered fields and perfumed paths,
So seeking solace in your cradled countryside
And my halcyon thoughts of home.

Isabelle Morgan Michalakis

MEMORIES

Looking back on Hatfield, the town in which I grew,
I think of all the old things, compare them with the new.
We had no Galleria and no Tesco super-store,
But in the street where I grew up we never locked a door.
We didn't have the *Social* but no child was left alone,
And help was always close at hand, we didn't need the 'phone.
Jack Oldings made the tractors, DeHavilland the planes,
And then, of course, in Beaconsfield, they took care of the trains.
We had a proper station and the buses were all green,
And the daffodils in Hatfield Park, made a most fantastic scene.
The engines on the test bed they ran both day and night,
And oh how very proud we were at the Comet's first test flight.
It was really good to live here, though we were *out in the sticks*
We didn't have the Forum, but we could go to the flicks.
We had no dead town centre, it was just St Albans Road,
Where they sold the things we needed, though it wasn't *A la Mode*.
We children were not angels, but we daren't be very bad,
'Cos anyone who caught us would go and tell our Dad.
It can't be quite the same now, with so many on the dole,
But how I miss the good old days, when Hatfield had a soul.

Isabel Beckwith

SURREY

Rolling hills and fields of green
The loveliest scenery I've ever seen
There's lots to see and plenty to do
It's a wonderful place, quite historical too

Mother nature abounds with the magic she makes
Streams full of trout and shimmering lakes
Woods and wildlife at every turn
Wild flowers and butterflies, fungi and fern

To get up early and don warm boots
Go down to the river amongst ducklings and coots
Is always a wonder I love to renew
To see pearls of moisture masquerading as dew

Gathering blackberries for crumbles and pies
An innocent pleasure as the summer dies
Then hazel and chestnuts to roast by the fire
A pastime of which I could never tire

Out in the countryside feeling so free
With peace all around is contentment for me
To meander forever among all that is good
I'd stay there for always if only I could

So please take your time and try not to hurry
If you have the chance to explore glorious Surrey
After a few tranquil rambles you'll surely agree
The county of Surrey is the best place to be.

Jo Fairclough

MY LOVELY MOTHER

A precious mother so warm and bright
her lovely face so full of grace.

When I feel low, she's always there
to listen advise and yes, to care.

She's one in a million, we are so close
my beautiful mother so kind and sweet
she's a pleasure for everyone to meet.

Her personality is full of life
my father says 'She's a wonderful wife.'

She's sixty six - you'd never know
her skin so young and all aglow.

Thank heavens for mothers they are so dear
your very best friend through all the
years, who helped wipe away those silly
tears.

And when I marry and have my own,
I'd like to think I'll be like mum,
enjoy my life and have some fun.

Pamela E Heath

LIFE IN CROYDON

Old town's full of streets and ghosts,
hearing old stories the bit I love most.

The church with its steeple, the market and
shops, a library of books, it's really the tops.

The gardens, the parks, theatres and schools,
there's something for everyone, it's where prosperity
rules.

The hospitals, fire stations are there if you need,
beware there's a police station, so villains take
heed!

The cars and the buses and motorbikes too,
Soon we'll have trams, now there's something new.

Cinemas, sports centres bursting with fun,
Swimming pools, football grounds where games can
be won.

The Mayor and his lady and royalty too,
Models and actors, to name but a few.

The rich and the famous, some come from here,
Some move away, but some have stayed near.

Life in Croydon is really the best, come
over and join us, put it to the test!

Leanne Simon

BOATS ON THE WEY NAVIGATION

They lie along the river bank
And hibernate beneath the trees,
As if for comfort, huddling close,
Resisting cruel winter's freeze.

When icy winds sweep past their bows
They nudge a little, shift and sigh,
Then sink back into sleep again,
Oblivious to passers - by.

But, spruced up, painted, engines tuned,
They're ready for those sunny days
When happy people climb aboard
To cruise down peaceful waterways.

Not far away a rotting hulk
Lies long abandoned, half submerged.
In driving rain it creaked and groaned
When round it swirling water surged.

A sad reminder of the past
When barges carried coal and grain
From Weybridge down to Guildford town,
Before the coming of the train.

Then fam'lies lived and worked on board,
And even children played their part.
But life was hard, the hours long,
And bargemen made an early start.

Now lorries rumble round our roads
And vans zoom down the motorway,
For speed is all, the pace is fast,
But is life better, who can say?

Gene Catherall

PAST AND PRESENT

I was born in Kennington
at the end of the Lambeth Walk,
Saturday night's supper was two pennyworth of pease pudding
and a slice of pickled pork.
Across Lambeth Bridge was all the sights,
Big Ben, Whitehall, Westminster Abbey too
and for a few pence on a London bus
I could visit the gardens at Kew.
But then when I got married
I moved to Carshalton, down in Surrey,
And to return to dear old London
I wasn't in a hurry.
I can stroll down to the *Oaks Park*
where I've spent many happy hours,
For there I can enjoy the squirrels,
the birds, the trees, the flowers.
I can catch a bus to Sutton
where there are many things to see,
The church, the library, the precinct,
they all appeal to me.
Then it's back to Carshalton Beeches
for that's where I want to be,
But the funny thing is, there is no sand
and neither is there any sea.

Irene Wales

LONDON BORN

A Cockney-lassie I was born
Within the year '07 -
Of working-class - salt of the earth -
My parents gifts from Heaven.

Ours was a little happy home
Where love was never far,
To me those years of long ago
Are as a guiding star.

Their love was something beautiful -
Alas - of length too brief,
When my dad died - it was as though
N'ere had there been such grief.

But time does take away deep pain,
It brings with it relief:
My mother smiled again - and I -
I had firmer belief.

Then came the war of thirty-nine -
We lost dear friends - our home,
But other friends of kindliness -
Made sure we did not roam.

Now I am left these many years,
Of goodly years am I;
Soon - soon will come the call for me
To quietly say good-bye.

A Cockney-lassie I was born, -
London long left behind; -
And yet - how proud I am to be
One of the Cockney-kind.

M L Lewin

REMEMBER WHEN YOU COULD STROLL AND BROWSE?

Do you remember Newbury as a market town?
A place to stroll and browse around
Where you could park and meet up with a friend
And not be driven round the bend!
Where you could stop and look and even choose.
All there is now is banks and shoes!
To get there is an absolute pain
Oh - not the A34 blocked again!
There's queues of cars and tons of lights
It's all unpleasant - quite a fight.
And, if you've finally managed to park,
What is there when all's said and done?
Shopping is no longer fun.
You cannot buy flour or a packet of salt
Surely somewhere someone's at fault.
Remember not everyone has a car
It's just not on to walk so far.
If you want food there is a free bus
But that doesn't suit all of us.
We just want to shop and buy what we please
Not struggle on buses with bags round our knees!
We do not like seats, shrubs and all those humps.
All of us shoppers are down in the dumps
Thank God good old Tesco is opening a store
There will be so many shoppers you won't see the floor!
But we've still got to get there.
And now the road's put on hold
I fear that man Mawhinney has been really bold
If he dares to come here he'd better look out
There's a whole lot of people after his blood!

Ann Holloway

OLD BOROUGH, YOUTHFUL SURREY - TODAY AND YESTERDAY!

Is there hope for our youngsters in Surrey,
Or is there cause to fret and worry?
Of any age at any pub, there seems little hope,
For they give fresh meaning to potplants and dope;
Versed in violent video values and computer bound,
There's surely no chance of character sound?

Half a century ago it was fishing in the Thames,
With hopscotch and *alleys* and lots of team games -
Rambles, runs and picnics, and dear old Chessington Zoo;
And such fun with those YC's, Young Socialists and Liberals too!
While Wilsons of Purley I know'll keep the prize
For a two-and-thruppenny treat, their old *sausage and mash and Jelly surprise!*

As youngsters in Malden, mum's perennial fuss
Was: 'Go nowhere near that ghastly Kingston by-pass!'
Today's mums have Ms 3 and 23 - and that M25,
Halving time from Godstone to Guildford, if you can stay alive.
Then compare Bentall's marvel, that first moving stairway,
With jetting round the world from Gatwick in just one day!

What else is new in Surrey, a generation later?
Well, there's two new prisons, where hospitals catered;
The Oaks have now gone, since the '87 storm,
But *The Derby* and Epsom are still there on form.
And Croydon's still a centre for a good shopping spree,
Albeit some say, 'At night, 'tis as dead as can be!'

My two sisters left for Canada in '56,
And two daughters married in Cumbria and Essex,
But four sons remain near us in Woodmansterne Lane,
Only one with that problem of computer migraine -
And, all told, they believe Surrey county and this country's the best,
Quite peaceful and civilised compared with the rest!

Adrian Arnold

MEMORIES OF FIR LODGE, CHURT

Oh, if a cherished wish you'd grant,
Then on some April morn,
Take me back to the dear old woods,
And house where I was born.

There in the realm of childhood days,
I'll wander all day long,
And find content in memories,
And in the blackbird's song.

But leave me there to my own will,
Nor by my side remain,
I want to be a child once more,
And tread those paths again.

So through the fields, into the woods,
And up the sandy lane,
I'd traversed many times to school,
In sunshine and in rain.

And there anemones I'll pick,
Wood violets by the score,
Primroses too, and buttercups
As in the days of yore.

And shall I find each treasured thing,
I wonder can it be?
That by the garden gate still grows
The double red May tree.

E Mumford

TRAPPED!

Surrey's a rat-race, it fills me with gloom,
So wearing you'd scarcely believe it.
I really don't like it, there's not enough room,
I'm wondering why I don't leave it.

Threats of redundancy fill us with dread
With interest rates rising and falling,
And asthma confines little children to bed
Since the traffic pollution's appalling.

The M25 is the best part for me,
A high-speed escape route from Surrey,
Well signposted, easy and smooth as can be,
No hassles, no problems, no worry.

O yes - there are cones and those contraflow lanes,
No loos, so you'd better not need 'em,
But drawbacks are greatly outnumbered by gains
On this highway to heavenly freedom.

Just turn left at Wisley and carry straight on
Past Heathrow and Chalfont St Peter;
You'll soon forget Surrey along the M1
And find other places much sweeter.

I've done it so often, this getting away
To calmer spots, fresh and appealing,
But after no more than a week and a day
I get this strange home-sickness feeling . . .

It must be my cats and my house and my friends
That pull me back here in a hurry;
I guess I'll be stuck here till life itself ends,
Ensnared by a county called Surrey.

Barbara Couvela

HORSELL VILLAGE SHOW

The doors were wide open
And with a deadline to beat,
The entrants arrived
With a challenge to meet.

With armfuls and boxes
They all hurried in,
With a hope it's their entry
That's going to win.

With a finishing touch
Their items they laid,
And then placed the card
For entry fee paid.

It was left then to the Judges,
To look, taste and choose,
For some would become winners
And others lose.

In the hall was much to view
Flowers, plants and cookery too,
But what gave all so much pleasure,
Had been made during leisure.

In the basement below,
With the veg and some fruit,
Were the children's entries,
Which looked quite cute.

The prizes were then given,
And we left the hall,
Knowing the success of next year,
Would depend on us all.

Derek J Williams

PICNIC AT RICKMANSWORTH

Waters meet,
rivers cross canals
and with other rivers blend.
Ponds drain to lakes,
lakes gurgle into rich green ditches and wend
their lazy way to swifter streams, flowing low
and lake feeds lake, that quietly rests below.

All these a wonderment,
part created, part made by man,
recalling miniature Persian works of irrigation
in a garden of The Oman.

There once upon a rich carpet,
spread beneath an olive gnarled,
did we partake
of fresh cut carrots,
served by the ancient gardener at the behest
of my host, the Sheikh.

So too can a frugal outdoor meal,
e'en here in leafy Hertfordshire,
a poet's banquet make.

Sidney John Wynn-Simmonds

GHOSTS OF PAST LIFE IN BUCKINGHAMSHIRE

Beneath the golden ball
Lies hidden secrets from days past
When wicked laughter echoed through West Wycombe caves
As members of the Hell-Fire Club met for nights of
    drunken revelry.
But hark! Listen to the great orator, Benjamin Disraeli,
As his words float across Hughenden Park,
The sweet smell of primroses filling the air
To remind us of Queen Victoria's visit.
As you journey through the beech tree valley,
See Milton at his Chalfont cottage
Or Shelley writing at his desk as the River Thames
    flows past his Marlow home.
Close your eyes and hear bodgers making the famous
    Windsor chairs,
Then listen to the whispers as John Hampden and friends
    meet to discuss the ship money levied by Charles I,
And what political secrets could the walls of Chequers reveal?
Feel the comradeship of the Buckinghamshire men who were
    tragically killed in the South African war
But still remembered by the monument at the top of Coombe Hill
The highest point in the Chilterns.
Then say a silent prayer as Buckinghamshire rests beneath the
    shadow of Whiteleaf Cross
Its past ghosts sleeping soundly as it faces tomorrow's dawn.

Patricia O'Gorman

COME TO WINDSOR

Windsor's more than just a castle
Awesome though that building is
State apartments quite the finest
Overseen by good Queen Liz.

Down the road there's Eton College
Home to all the toffs you know
See them in their fancy get-ups
Boarding there - it takes some dough.

In the town a first-class theatre
Restaurants for every taste
Shops galore for you to browse in
You will have no time to waste.

Just outside we have a racecourse
Where you'll find the Sport of Kings
Picturesque beside the river
Go and see what your luck brings.

On the river you can cruise to
Maidenhead or Boulters Lock
Take it easy, put your feet up
Even snooze before you dock.

Worth a visit Windsor Great Park
Maybe watch the polo there
Follow this with Savill Garden
Gorgeous plants, so many rare.

Come to Windsor we do beg you
History awaits you here
Better than the hurried day trip
Stay with us - it won't be dear.

Richard Lewis

WATFORD

Fraying hem of the metropolis,
Not countryside or cosmopolitan.
Slipped into some deep coma,
Grey with boredom and winter rain.
Soulless shopping centre of the masses.
Purveyor of sod all to the middle classes.
With its wide range of narrow minds,
Off the shelf lifestyles,
And thoughtless crimes.
Rotting in its own antipathy,
To culture, lust, its own mistrust.
Its people shuffle off to disappointing lovers,
Seeking slices of light,
Buried under dark and cloudy covers,
As if weighed down,
With the general anticlimax of life.
A weak assemblage of cement and stone,
Euphemistically known,
When I tried to leave it,
As my home.
Having no sin, I'll cast the first stone.
Smash it down,
Raze this prison to the ground,
And escape towards life,
Beyond ten thousand entrapped fates.
The pond stagnates.

Robert Woollard

EPSOM TOWN CENTRE

Through Epsom Town I wend my way
On a cold but sunny Saturday.
People mingle in the street
Jostling elbows and clumsy feet,
Hearing snatches of conversations
There are so many variations.
Some shops have closed down
It's hard to survive
In the year nineteen hundred and ninety five.
How obvious it is to see
We have no classless society,
Poor people not dressed to beat the cold
With shoulders bent are mostly old.
Parents with children, no affluence here
The cost of living is too dear.
Their faces show tension they cannot hide
Reflecting depressions they feel inside.

Staff from the banks are full of fun
Laughing they pass me one by one,
Young and trendy they make their way
Into a pub, it's now midday.

Then I see the well-to-do confident
And so well groomed,
The world to them must feel sublime
Their lives much sweeter than any wine.

Sylvia Reddick

COOTERS HILL FARM
HARPENDEN

The tousled headed trees
Entwine the sloping roofs
Of the nestling farm
Against the autumnal
Pink tinged fading light
All - a breathless calm;
A picture often seen
On fly - leaf cover
Calendar and glossy magazine,
One that never fades
A simple English scene
Of varying lights and shades
Just to gaze upon to find
Sweet solace and healing balm
For the busy harassed mind.

David Howell

EAST ILSLEY

Oh how my heart longs for all of those familiar landmarks
Old hedgerows, older tracks, that lead to rolling downs and skylarks,
There I would open wide my eyes and gently flood my brain
With images of past, to drown this ever-present pain.

I know your fields, the very earth I've crumbled in my fingers
The Sunday sound of your church bells, still, in my memory lingers
Long strings of horses, breathing smoke, the lads, slumped, almost sleeping
Sixpenny hops on Saturdays, my parents in your keeping.

The Star, the Sun, the Swan, the Lamb, the ancient Crown and Horns
That bush in Snellers' garden, with its deadly triple thorns.
Still there, loves of my childhood, still there for me to find.
I write no more, emotion chokes and tears have made me blind.

Robert Arnold

GARDEN SWEET

I love my garden, my garden loves me
I love the sunlight as it bursts through the trees.
Early I rise and alone shall I be,
There are no other humans I company or seek.

So peaceful this early as I drift along,
Sounding nature's ensemble dawn chorus, the song.
My hedgerow is home, tiny the wren
Bindweed and grasses to pull now and then.

Keeping the bees but a finger away,
As I separate weeds, this summer's morning to stay.
Planting and fussing changing my style
For all this hard work walking mile after mile.

I love my garden, my garden loves me
Sweet are the moments spending with thee.

Benson

DOWN THE LAKE

Sunday afternoons amble
down the lake, St Albanians
All.
Talking, looking, feeding -
ice-cream licking -
Flirting, coupling,
Wildlife and all!

Pamela Bley

HE IS CALLED MAYHO

He is called Mayho, and on the wings of a prayer,
To our Surrey town he came from blood-soaked Sarajevo.
And as surely as the Downs do roll, this quiet man
Has touched the face of our suburban town and warmed its soul.

Come now to his wife, who these three years has struggled through
The most pain-wracked, desolate years of her life.
And to his daughter and son reunite, this brave man
Has brought his fatherly care and turned to sunny day a family's dark night.

He says it is good, our bustling, every-day Surrey town.
He marvels at the sharp, fresh air, the electric lights, the buses, the food.
He rediscovers water out of a tap, for in the war back home
It is fourteen flights up with buckets of water, then fourteen flights back.

'Wonderful!' he cries, when he sleeps a whole silent night through,
And then watches the pale winter sun ascend through smokeless skies.
For back home in the war, the nights pass in wary terror of what happens next and
The sun is shrouded in a constant haze of acrid smoke, the colour of blood and gore.

And in our high road, he lingers long by the corner and gazes right and left,
Staring at restaurants and shops, but not to admire their menus or modes.
He marvels at the glass, the yards of window that remain intact and clear
For the windows of Sarajevans are all gaping holes, through which all elements pass.

He is a hero. For being brave and tough and determined and lucky
His reward it two short months in Surrey, out of Sarajevo.
But horrific to think that at the end of this respite from unending hell
Back he'll go - into the morass of human suffering, there again to sink.

He is called Mayho. And on the wings of a prayer
To our Surrey town he came from blood-soaked Sarajevo.
Richer we for knowing this man. For we now know our town for what it really is:
Nestled calm against the Surrey Downs, a place of peace, in a fine, free land.

Kathy Oliver

A WINTER BIRTH

Feeble foal spilled into a frosty morning
Patient mare melts icicles as they form.
Strangely the stables had no warning.
White tipped grass and glinting frost
The sun shines deeply from its bluw awning.
Grey church tower lit with ice
Black trees strike powerless against its burning.
Quiet and still the pair, the mare
Stands unsurprised and calm.
The foal twists his neck to see her, yearning
For the warm safe cocoon lost in his borning.
First hunger stirs, the shaky legs grow firm
With milk he feels his first strength churning.
The mare accepts, then walks ahead
Unmoved, resigned to a new life's dawning.

Sylvia J Goodman

BEDDINGTON

Beddington boot sales with
Beddington bells;
Beddington bustle and bridges;

Beddington waters; the
willow tipped Wandle
beguiling both walkers and watchers.

Beddington manor, dove-
coted Carew, lends
open air concerts, charisma.

Beddington rural, where
Raleigh once rode, of
lavender fields it once
boasted.

Beddington's present and
Beddington's past;
Beddington's pride in its riches;

Beddington's villagers
vowing to blend an
historical view with new vistas.

Joan Amor

HERTFORDSHIRE LIFE - 1995

While Hertfordshire's past is being protected
New buildings and complexes are being erected
Conservationists protest at the loss of Green Belt
But with careful planning, no loss is felt;
Some of the country's best gardens are found
In many of Hertfordshire's old and new towns.

Whether you live in the country, a village or town
There're buses and coaches to get you around
Along *B* roads and *A* roads the dual carriage-ways
And the prime of them all - the fast motorways.
And for those who don't like long traffic delays
There is usually a train to take them away.

A priority is always a good education
In which Hertfordshire is one of the tops of the nation
Though lacking in Unis. - this is inconsequential -
A good basic primary is far more essential.

Hertfordshire was severely hit by recession
for quite a long time there was a general depression
When industry took quite a hard knock.
You'll find that most new buildings are just office blocks
Long after completion some remain empty -
Offices To Let - these signs are plenty.

Hertfordshire homes are not very cheap
Making mortgage repayments hard to keep.
So in this year of '95
Some may struggle to survive
While others on their laurels rest
And think Hertfordshire Life is the very best!

Jean Hunter

A PLACE I CALL HOME

I wasn't born in Bushey,
But to me it is my home,
I saw it landmarked on the map,
And from my nest I've flown.

Anything your heart desires,
You'll find within its paths,
A shop to purchase Kite-Kat,
A pub for booze and laughs.

Shop-keepers always have a word,
To them you are a friend,
Pass on idle chatter,
And a listening ear they'll lend.

The scene down Bushey High Street,
If an artist, I would paint,
Antique shops that bulge with memories,
Along with cottages so quaint.

The duck pond by the churchyard,
Is a joy for all to see,
The ducks perform a cabaret,
Take a seat - it's all for free!

See them waddle off in anger,
When they loose the fight for bread,
Nagging at the giving hand,
If their open beaks not fed.

The beauty that surrounds you,
Is such that should be known,
I'm proud to say I've seen it,
That's why Bushey is my home.

Trudy Sunderland

WE WERE THE OVALTINEYS

Hazy fields of Mitcham lavender, spreading to the common's edge,
The River Wandle, cool and clear, meanders through the watercress-beds.
Clutching tight the fishing-net, the child hangs from the bridge's ledge,
Chasing clouds of sticklebacks, never heeding where she treads.
A slippery stone, a reach too far,
A splash that damps the fine spring day;
Slopping home with one wet foot; whatever will her mother say?
Hot and humid in the scullery, always fraught on washing day,
Heedless of the silvery fishes, swimming in the little jar.

Sink and scrubber, old hand mangle, cobbles making draining poor,
Carbolic soap and elbow grease, the overalls are washed once more.
Unnoticed in the steamy melee, the wetted-one slides out the door.
She's free again, she grabs her trike, *her heel is rubbed a little sore,*
She pedals fast along the lane, untroubled by the single car.
Down to the ford again she scrambles,
Scratching face amongst the brambles,
Along the banks she slips and ambles,
Always at the Rivers' bar.

Then the evening, home for tea,
Bottled pears from nanma's tree.
Hissing wireless by the fire; Ovaltiney Song for me,
Radio Luxembourg fading, fading; *a valve is going, just you see.*
Sitting there by glowing gas-light, snoozing dog with twitching paw,
Fresh from washing at the tap
Dad will take a well-earned nap,
Mum with darning in her lap,
All is peaceful 'til she sees, one damp print upon the floor.

Pat Knight

WELWYN

Could you linger a while, down Welwyn way,
Maybe visit, stay more than a day.
A village so quaint and clean,
The shops are now so rarely seen.
They are closing down and being moved on.
Villagers so sorry to see them all gone.

The river runs on, under the road,
In it swims ducks, fish and a toad,
All hiding away as people rush by,
Reflecting the birds as they fly in the sky.
A little school, a church on a hill,
Why can't progress just stand still.

Further on and up the hill,
Great woods, now stand so silent and still.
In all autumn glory to catch your eye,
So ancient and beautiful, they're triple SI
But chainsaws came, shattered the peace,
Down came the trees, cutting did not cease.

Until years of old wood, all lay in a pile,
The sale of the wood, making profits smile.
People in high places, who said this is right,
Don't hear the people who cry in the night.
It's just like vandalism, done legal by man,
Sure, it's not right, but prove it, who can.

J Ladley

SEASONS

Access for all, to this idyllic place
A national park, with beauty and grace,
To give rest and joy, peace, and relief,
Yet the best of all, 'tis my belief
While seasons may come, as times pass,
Exmoor's valley, forever will last.

Spring awakes, as birds at dawn
Drink from the waters, so fast and torn,
Foaming white, cascading down
From hills and vales all around.
See flowers appear in colours proud
Nodding to nature, in her soft green gown.

Hear the waters, sing in summer's hue
Rippling and turning, washing stones anew,
In sunlight bright, or through shaded nook
The sound of music, from a bubbling brook,
Our tapestry of life, all is here
Of ages past, or still to appear.

Autumn brings, soft amber and gold
To trees and banks, life's story told,
As waters slow, where leaves are falling
Back to earth, her centuries calling,
For sleep prepare, to rest once more,
As in the valley, we love to explore.

Deep in winter, this lovely vale
Shows us her beauty, along a trail,
Snow falling gently, yet washed away
As we traverse the waters, cold and grey.
Now running quietly clear and deep
While nature is at her rest and sleep.

Muriel Elder

SUTTON TOWN

Often I think of the beautiful town
That is seated by the country
The pleasant streets of that dear old town
And my youth comes back to me.

I can see the shadowy lines of the trees,
Churches, cottages, over-grown gardens.
Children playing in the park.
Mothers out shopping with their babies.

Local folk and visitors come
To the library, to the arts
Pubs, restaurants, cinemas
Come and visit our town
And you will see what it
Means to me.

Old brick schools you will see.
The children have a happy
Interest in the borough just like me.

In our Sutton town
There is time to think, read
Paint and draw. Lots to do and see
So come and have fun.

Valerie Ryan

THE HERTFORD ANTIQUES FAIR

The crick grows in my neck
and am I tired of walking circles!
One day yet
I'll remember to turn left instead of right
My eyes are double glazing
Behind the glamour-daze, still gazing
Always shuffle, linger, shuffle
'til the yearning gets too strong

Till the burning gets too pungent
and the odour of the spot lamps
is a dusty kind of sickness
falling soft as snowflakes falling
while the money changes hands . . .

Then the guilty daze of spending
leaves me aching, slow awaking
One day
I will remember to turn left instead of right . . .
Now I stumble home, bags bulging
from the freedom of indulging
Free from shuffling in circles -
'til the next fair comes along

Hez

WOODLAND FANTASY

I've walked the quarry woods today
The sun in lovely golden beams
Hit moss strewn tree stumps on my way
And suddenly recalled my dreams.

Those lovely dreams of yester year
When I was young and sent to look
For toad and mole, they seemed so near
Those friends from Kenneth Grahame's book.

Where ever one may roam today
Through Berkshire with its meadows green
Its woods and forests seem to say
Just look, and wild wood friends are seen.

Wind in the Willows will always be
In tune with Berkshire's many scenes,
I'm sure the author will ever see,
Where Toad and Mole have always been.

Joyce Cooper

IN THE ABBEY

Will the sea swirl
Through those round rock arches?
Did waves once batter
Where the window walls them off?
Here is my shelter
For the storms to come,
Here led my path
And brought me home.

Ruth Partington

THE NORTH DOWNS

The Downs the countryside,
You're free
To walk the fields
Wild birds to see.

The North Downs cover
Many miles.
O'er vales and hills,
And over stiles.

St. Marthas on the hill,
History in store.
Travel to Guildford
For lots lots more.

Dorking with its caverns
Down below.
Shere and Peaslakes
Summer Show.

Woking rather flat,
You say.
Good theatre.
London way.

Chertsey, Staines,
M25.
Thorpe Park shuts
At half past five.

Routes to North
And sunny South.
Surrey's mine,
By word of mouth.

Rosemary J Povey

DINTON PASTURES

Away from the bustle and noise of the street
A short car ride brings us this peaceful retreat.
A leisurely stroll, with some casual talk
Just the ingredients for an evening's walk.
Before us lie lakes, as smooth as glass
Reflecting sky and clouds drifting past.
Yachts skim the water like birds on the wing
Not feathers, but sails gently flapping.
Small bridges to cross and winding paths
Bordered by the greenest of grass.
Ducks, swans and geese are everywhere
Like us enjoying the warm evening air.
If we pause, they surround us, hoping to share
Whatever we've got which isn't a lot.
Our feast is before us, not for stomachs, but eyes
For wonderful colours have lit up the skies
The huge golden sun is shedding its ray
A final goodbye to what was the day.
We end our walk as dusk draws nigh
And turn to whisper a last goodbye.
To this oasis of nature which brings such delight
But it has gone, claimed by the night.

Monica Jefferies

WINTER GOLF AT MOOR PARK

Across the frost-hard, ice-white greens,
A fairytale of fairway dreams,
Great white giants with sparkling sprays
Guard bunkers set in sandy waves.

Some gnome-like, bulky forms
Dream of summer's lush green lawns.
Vests, polos, woollies, wets,
Numbed lips and misty breath.

Icing crunch shoe-spikes stride
Across the winterland with pride,
Following their eternal quest -
Perfecting shots to beat the rest.

Fairy fur on frozen frond
Surrounds the fish-tombed, concrete pond.
Tingling fingers and chilly toes,
Red, chaffed cheeks and runny nose.

Moor Park's mansion contemplates
The optimists who pass her gates,
And wonders, when their task is done,
The golfers choice of winter fun!

Dinah Kane

DREAMS OF BERKSHIRE

Berkshire county leaves me breathless,
This heavenly vision in a valley.
From the top of green rolling Downs,
To the meandering Thames and Shallows.
Fairest Berkshire most royal county,
Here she stands in majestic splendour.
Etched with leaves and branches arching,
Held in lavish glowing colours.
From the highest stone built castle,
To the humblest brick built terrace,
It has it all in fine profusion
Just a glance and one must linger,
Here England in its richest patchwork,
Holding all the finest stables,
Where thoroughbreds are lively stepping,
Athletes born of fastest prowess
In most regal grandeur showing,
Shire filled with our army's budding leaders,
Old school ties, boaters, rowers,
College pupils taught to perfection,
Scientific minds abound in measure.
Glorious history in the making,
The past now laid out in wonder,
Passing faces from times preceding,
Catching at times unsuspecting.
Place of warmth and childhood, it's you
Leads my heart forever homeward.

Colleen Thatcher

PRECIOUS COUNTY

East Berks. the place where I was born
Now what I see, I only mourn
Urban blight stretching for miles
concrete roads concrete tiles
Vast estates and factories blight
a county that was my delight

Small villages and country towns
country lanes and lofty downs
go westward and they still survive
a rural Berkshire still alive
Wantage Ilsley Abingdon
The ridgeway strides across her down

Walk it, perhaps, all is not lost
Inkpen's head up in the mist
Winter hill, see Thames toll by
Lambourn, Kennet, Ladons stream
let us keep our county green
fight as if it were a duty so Berkshire may
retain some beauty

Howard Wallace Gibbs

THE WEIR ON THE RIVER THAMES

The river had flowed so peacefully on its way
With no hint of what was shortly in store.
The ducks bobbed on the tranquil water.
I followed the river along its bank.

What began as a gentle noise grew
As I drew closer into a mighty roar
As the water possessed tumbled over itself
Changing into a white foaming mass.

This powerful flood deafened my ears.
Why had the gentle water turned so savage?
It bubbled like a witch's cauldron.
Water in turmoil. Water in confusion.

Cascading violently to its lower level.
Then at first gradually calming
Until its struggle was finally over
And the river flowed gently once more.

What a majestic sight the weir was.
Never ceasing through day and night.
Transforming peacefulness and calm
Into a crescendo of excitement.

The weir held a fascination for me.
What a wonderful part of the river it was.

John Christopher Cole

BED-SIT SURREY

From the twenty-twenty vision of my Epsom solitude
Hoarding thought to keep my brain alive,
Starving greedy memory of sentimental food
To allow a little logic to survive.

From the steady cultivation of an absent mindedness
To keep some recollections out the act,
Thus in cleaning down a surface or clearing up a mess
Such choring leaves my sanities intact.

From a past so downright vicious that to keep it in its place
Superhuman insulation's are required,
Lest it breaches my pretences and grins into the space
That gaped when all the gods I had, expired.

So, from a nightmare to a nightmare as I rise at four o'clock
Any infiltrating memories to trample,
Though mayhem has to be complete, I weep as I take stock
Of *one* mangled casualty inside the sample.

Neville Wray

PRINCE CHARLES IN CROYDON

When Prince Charles came to Croydon
In November 1994
He found a market full of folk
All British to the core
He chatted with them
Tried their wares
And perhaps for just a while
Forgot his worries and his cares.
Maybe one day, when Charles is King.
And things are looking good
He'll remember his visit to Croydon
And the market where he stood.

Frances Powell

WHEN VILLAGE RAILWAYS DIED

Along disused track
Builder's stock lies scattered
In confusion of concrete,
Crazy cluttered tiles,
Corner-crumbled bricks,
Unplumbed pipes, porcelain
And horizontal doors.
Here nettles droop dull green
Over blinded window panes as
Malignant elder creeps
Through sleepers cast aside
And rails prized up,
When village railways died.

David Ayres

THE GROVE, CARSHALTON

There is a bit of paradise in old Carshalton town,
It's the place that you should visit if you are feeling down.
Stroll along by the river, past lush lawns and flower beds
And drink in the many colours, blues, yellows, pinks and reds;
Or, if wildlife's your pleasure, there are lots of woodlands round
Where trees, wild-flowers, squirrels and birds of all kinds abound.
Look across at the island, there are water-birds galore;
Swans and ducks, Canadian geese and many, many more.
Then stand upon the wooden bridge, gaze at the waterfall
Tumbling down those rocky steps, it's a sight that will enthral.
There's so much more that I could say, but words I cannot find
For all the many wondrous thoughts this place puts in my mind.
I'm sat now on the waterfront, watching the world go by,
Thinking what they're all missing - and oh how lucky am I!

Daphne Lodge

SURBITON

Oh! Surbiton, Suburban Queen,
So many changes you have seen;
Victorian mansions, now pulled down,
Once used to grace this pleasant town.

> Before the day the railway came
> The town was quiet - few knew its name.
> But Kingston would not have the trains.
> To us they came, and for our pains
> The town then prospered, quickly grew.
> Stockbrokers, bankers, merchants, knew
> A better place to live by far,
> Then EC4 or Potters Bar.

Oh! Surbiton, Suburban Queen,
So many changes you have seen.
Two cinemas once flourished here
And now there's none. Who sheds a tear?

> The stately steeple of St. Mark's
> Stands proudly after Hitler's sparks
> Destroyed our church, which rose again,
> A testament to toil and pain.
> A childhood memory I have stowed,
> Of sheep, in Queen Victoria's Road.
> In Crocker's Yard the steaming drays
> Moved tons of coal for wint'ry days.

Oh! Surbiton, Suburban Queen,
So many changes you have seen.
But Thames flows on at tranquil pace.
The riverside's a pleasant place.

Heather Claridge

MY HOME TOWN

Just outside this town I live
With pretty streets looking also neat
A fine old church stands in the town
Built of flint and looking proud

22 years and I've come to know
This old place that I call my home
Rickmansworth is where it is
The best place that I have ever lived

There's everything a man could want
With parks and rivers and the aquadrome
Canals with boats just floating by
What a lovely sight to catch ones eye

It does not matter where I go
The people here all say 'Hello'
As I walk down through the street
So many people and friends I meet

A walk through the park or down the stream
A friendly face you will always see
It does not matter where you go
The people here still say 'Hello'

I love this place that I call my home
And all the people I've come to know
They're all so friendly and I can see
They all love this town just like me.

Barry Vincent

CARSHALTON

You would love Carshalton
with its park so green
to see the beauty of the swans
Swimming through the breeze.
Many times I take a walk
that leads me to the ponds
to gaze upon the Cenotaph
of those we loved and lost.
Further on there's Honeywood
Lodge, built so strong and proud
it only cost just 60 pence
to have a look around.
The billiard room, musician room
makes one feel so proud.
Our village neat, so very sweet
many friends one often meets
to see them smile, talk a while
so come to Carshalton it's a treat.

Phyllis St. John-Fuller

HERTS.

I've lived in Herts. for many years
It's here I've realised
All my hopes, all my fears.

In my youth
Around here was quiet.
To tell you the truth
Maybe too quiet.

The countryside is pretty
Trees, flowers and such.
Through the years concrete and putty
Have changed things with their ugly touch.

Motorways have sprung up everywhere.
Traffic moving, no time to spare.
No time to sit and stare
At beautiful Hertfordshire.

I don't think I'll stray
It's here I'll stay
Though changes have been made.
It's my home, in Herts, where once I played.

Margaret Lewis

HOGSNORTON

Do you remember down the lane
Hogsnorton used to be
Well years ago we lived there
My family and me

Four cottages once stood there
For all the world to see
Four families once lived there
It was nineteen forty three

We walked to school across the field
Just up by Hodge's Farm
Our gas mask bag and sandwiches
We carried on our arm

The copper in a little shed
Stood just across the yard
Our mother boiled the clothes in there
Yes times were very hard

The Gypsies in their caravans
Who lived just down Slip Lane
They all worked out in Hodge's Fields
In sunshine snow and rain

Our mother worked in fields with them
We children helped there too
We picked potatoes stacked the corn
There was so much to do

Now when I am all alone
Remembering way back then
I wish my mum was here with me
And we could start again

C Beatty

ROSE COTTAGE

The night was still, there was a bright full moon
Mist hung around the lane like a thick black cloak
An owl shrieked and sent a shiver down my spine
From my toes to my head, I felt that I might choke

A dwelling with thatched roof by name Rose Cottage
Stood like a fortress in the pale moon beams
Throwing a shadow over all, in its beauty
Was a place where you could have your wildest dreams

I imagined I could see a figure creeping up the lane
He had a patch over one eye and a scarf on his head
Was pushing a barrel there was sweat on his brow
I did not approach him, or I might be dead

They were a rowdy crowd that followed him
But this cottage was their new hiding place
These smugglers had some plans tonight
Somewhere to shelter, a place they would be safe

Margaret Rose Davies

HEART OF THE LAND

The Hertfordshire stag runs on its way
From early in the morning till the end of the day,
A stream flows softly as it runs through the creak
Past the old country villages so pretty, so chic.
The horses in the field standing and grazing,
In the Hert's countryside, so green and amazing,
Long country walks through fields and the trees,
Feel the wind in your hair from a slight summers breeze.
Country fayres in churches and halls,
And the red leaves laying as Autumn falls,
This is Hertfordshire the heart of the land,
And God could have blessed it with his own hand.

Alan Pine

WINDSOR CASTLE

Windsor Castle, standing strong and bold,
From miles around you can behold
Towers and walls of noble fame
The *Standard* flying, royalty's name,
Now in the area is some alarm
That Windsor soon may lose its charm,
If oil rigs stand near the Great Park
Drilling, the deer would swiftly embark.

Although the Great Fire played a part
In robbing Windsor of its heart
If they turn the grounds to sludge
Windsor folk would bear a grudge.
So keep Windsor town the tourists love
As it is, and do not move
Equipment there to spoil its grace
For oil wells only can deface.

And long may Windsor Castle stand
A stronghold, towering o'er the land,
Beloved by all who pass it by
Heritage and beauty, none can deny.
Though many intrigues there may be
Within the Royal Family,
They need no *Dallas* on the scene
Our *Dynasty* is just our Queen.

Joan Heybourn

HERTFORDSHIRE

A higher moment,
my soul dancing
within.

I gaze, bask, find
myself dreaming.
In the distance

you stand my love,
blowing kisses to
the trees

as a warm breeze
explores your golden
hair.

The woodlands respond,
whispering.
Dancing slightly.

O Hertfordshire,
what beauty is yours,
what love you breed.

Colin Gibson

EPSOM DOWNS

It's great to live in Epsom, especially on the Downs.
Miles of rolling country side, amidst so many towns.
We have our special memories, of grandchildren very small.
Picnics, kites, roly-poly, we had to do it all.

There is something here for every age,
A Leisure Centre for a swim, you can fly a model plane,
A place to park the car, or even use the train.

We have the well known Derby Day,
When champagne flows like water,
Punters, gamblers, the fair ground,
It does not really alter.

And when the crowds drift away,
The Downs get cleaned for another day.
So today is wet and cold, with mist among the trees.
Blue tits visit for the nuts. Squirrels quite a tease.

And even from the window, there is so much to admire.
The sky is always beautiful, different colours,
I can never tire.

This place is oh so special,
Right in the heart of Surrey
In fact it's *Surrey Life*
And said to have no worry!

Eileen S Clayton

A ROYAL COUNTY

It's a royal county this Berkshire
With a royal castle proud
In Windsor, whose streets are never complete
Without a seething crowd.

They stand and stare at the pageantry
Of ancient customs still used.
The soldiers march by. Overhead the 'planes fly,
While the people wander, bemused.

It's a royal county this Berkshire
Where royal race meetings are seen;
Where people dress up in their best bib and tuck,
To parade up and down, and to preen.

They cheer as the royal horse carriage
Goes by with its spanking team.
And it makes them feel proud to be part of the crowd
Who are there to hob nob with the queen.

It's a royal county this Berkshire
With a history centuries old.
There are ancient inns where the beer barrels brim
Once used by highwaymen bold.

There are flintstone churches still standing
Though built many centuries ago;
Where ancient old trees spread their branches in peace,
And the gravestones still stand in a row.

It's a royal county this Berkshire
With farms and hamlets and towns
Knit together as one by the Thames. In its sum
It's the heart of old England, its crown.

Louise Willoughby

COUNTY FAIR

Surrey is a county fair
With hills, woods, commons and rivers
Populated by those who care
To protect its attractions so diverse;
It is a county par excellence
As beautiful as any place per chance

From Thames border in the north
You are recommended to set forth
Your senses will enjoy a feast
Unable to decide what's best

Art galleries, theatres, museums too
Even theme parks and a zoo
Cater for those of various ages
With tastes intellectual, sports and crazes.

Nightingales sing in Staffhurst Woods
Inculcating happy moods
Mammals like dormice and weasels abound
With badgers and foxes underground

At Bay Ponds you'll find butterflies
As children dip for bugs they prize
Wild flowers profuse on Juniper Hill
Its sunsets glorious as air gets still

Epsom's known throughout the world
For Derby Day with flags unfurled
People come to see the horses
At birthplace of race courses

Richmond on Thames is a riviera
Promenades, cafes, boats together
Whatever you want Surrey can give
It's probably best place to live

C Bryant

A MISTY MORNING

A misty morning, cold and wet,
With low grey fog-cloud overhung,
'Twould make you miserable, and yet
How gladsomely I strode along.
A thrush beneath that leaden sky
Sang lustily his rapturous song
That breathed of Spring. -
'Margaret, Margaret, Margaret.'
So sang the thrush, or seemed to sing,
For through my brain those words did ring
As on I strode,
Spurning the miry puddles in the road,
Exulting in the mist and mocking at the rain
That drizzled down in vain
To damp the ardour of the bird's wild song
That sang aloud my joy for me.
For she was come whom I had missed so long,
And soon I would be with her face to face,
And oh! for me dull winter yielded place,
The mist, the rain, the cold, melted away,
And all was spring time with the joy of May.

Alwyn Trubshaw

ALWAYS THERE

When and if things can get worse
never despair
For you know I am always there
Not able to offer much
but just hold out my hand
Always being there
Wondering, wishing and hoping you still care
Only a fool could believe
there could never be no love between
You and me.
Always wanting and hoping for the best
Just letting you know I am still there
Always being there
Hoping for you, the best

Margaret A Bond

HARLEQUIN

Razzle - Dazzle -
Fab-U-matazzle
Harlequin's coming to town.

Sizzle - Fizzle -
I'm all a tizzle
Shopping for that special gown.

Buy it - Try it -
Electrify it
Twentieth century crown

Push it - Pull it -
Professionals through it
Silky smile - only failures frown.

Stephanie Scott

THE LONDON BOROUGH OF SUTTON

We're only a suburb?
We used to be *Surrey*!
But don't ever pass
Our charms in a hurry.

The borough of Sutton
Is pleasant and clean
We've prizes to prove it
The town is so keen!

Our parks are outstanding
Our Avenues treed
Our leisure attractions
Meet everyone's need.

The council's efficient
It listens to us
It spends money wisely,
Decides, without fuss

What's best for the people
Who've given it their trust.
I've lived here for ages
My praises are just!

Lilian Ruxton

SOLESBRIDGE LANE 1995

This is the place wherein I dwell,
A narrow lane, a crowd of trees,
A rising field, a woodland dell . . .
The song of traffic on the breeze.

A lane that turns and winds about,
Where blackthorn grows and snowy may;
And here a cottage, here a wood . . .
And here the teeming motorway.

The squirrels sport among the boughs
And hide the hazel nuts from sight,
The muntjac deer appear by day,
And foxes roam the place by night.

Reminders of an earlier day:
The Old Forge cottage near the top,
The whitewashed house not far away
That was the rural butcher's shop.

The Old Mill site upon whose ground
Some Roman relics here were found;
And on to Sarratt, down the lane . . .
We cross the motorway again!

A yaffle in the apple tree
Pecks insects from the rotting bark,
Nocturnal cats go silently
And do their hunting in the dark,

And nothing here will pause to stay
To hear the merry motorway.
And though it cuts across my view
I must confess . . . I use it too.

J Hubbard

HERITAGE?

Classy ladies from glossy magazines,
Gentlemen with tails eyeing the scene.
Heard noises of thunder but not from the sky,
Pounding the turf your hope gallops by.
So fill your glass with bubbles my dear,
Your ticket in silk has sped from the rear.
As the crowd grew ecstatic
History! Another king for a classic,
So excitement let loose with a cheer.
The lights now fading, tradition is too,
World famous on Wednesday now the weekend will do.
The giant that shone black is the star,
It is him they sought from near and afar.
So here is the most famous one and a half miles,
A sea of happy faces laughter and smiles,
Up high brilliant and so very white,
The Queen stands a regal site,
Keeping guards in single file,
Watching watching all the while.

Claire Knight

RICKMANSWORTH

I collapse into my seat on the busy Metro line,
living in London would be all very fine,
but as the train leaves that hubbub behind
and the track opens out into fields, I soon find,
the peace of the meadows and woodlands beyond,
in this Hertfordshire county of which I'm so fond,
is a welcoming sight after trudging around,
following the crowd on the Underground.
The canal with its longboats follows the track,
as it travels from Aldgate to Amersham and back.

I walk from the Station in Rickmansworth town.
It's a bit frayed at the edges, a little run down.
But where would you find a cosier place?
I worry that soon, it may not stand the pace,
with the great supermarkets taking custom away,
small shops open up, but don't seem to stay.
But I find that this town has one very rare,
quality about it that others don't share,
you can walk from the High Street and turn left or right,
go straight ahead, and you are in quite,
the most beautiful countryside stretching afar,
with bird song and wild life wherever you are.

Swans skim along on the shimmering lake,
like pure white clad skaters, food scraps to take.
Small boys and their dad's patiently wait,
with their camp stools, lunch boxes, small tins of bait,
along the canal bank with their rods at the ready.
'Don't fidget lad - keep your hands steady!'
It's amazing to think that a short trip away,
is the city of London I can visit any day.

Maureen Hembley

UNTITLED

At Hatch End set high,
The old folks sigh
For the green fields of long ago,
Where the tall trees leaned
Over chuckling streams
And the buttercups swayed and glowed.

These sights and sounds are now no more,
Instead - a continuous traffic roar.
What green is still there
We must all of us share
With hamburger wrappings and other litter
No wonder the old folks are sad and a little bitter.

Will there be change for the good
Oh we wish it would.
But with the demands of today.
Expect a gigantic highway!
From Ricky' in the west
To Stanmore no less.

A question expected from those not yet born
May very well be 'What is a lawn?'
They will probably think it a type of cement
When will those responsible relent?
If they do - once again a pleasant land
Where all can walk hand in hand.

R C Cook

A CAMEO VIEW OF THE HOME COUNTIES

Essex, Kent, Surrey, Hertfordshire, Home Counties ground
What a diversity of people and places abound
Well known is Essex girl and man
Where trends in politics are near to the ground
Kent is where sea breezes blow
Remnants of a Cockney dialect still flow
Also where the fruit trees grow
Canterbury is a Cathedral town
where dark deeds of history were done
Thomas a Beckett was murdered here
Roman Catholics were full of fear
Surrey is a suburban place
Many elegant houses are there on show
Royal Palaces and gardens full of grace
Hampton Court Palace, Kew Gardens to name but two
The deer roam in Richmond Park, a place to view
A traffic escape to tranquillity here
Time warped to bring to the eye a tear
Hertfordshire is somewhat heading North to pastures new
New towns grew here to take London population overflow
Meant to be a vision of planned perfection
Letchworth where industry and flowers were to grow
A county is a mixture of ancient and modern
St. Albans, Hatfield House, Stevenage
Thus the Home Counties trail is nearing its end
No further we will go, but just to send
Greeting to all the people in the area we know
You have missed lots out you cry
Alas brevity is to obey the rules
The gaps are in the inner eye

Margaret Fowler

DREAM ON

Those days of my boyhood,
Had so many great ambitions,
A successful career in football,
What ever the conditions.
My dreams of playing cricket,
Scoring centuries at Lords,
Taking wicket after wicket,
To enjoy so much applause.

Then performing on the stage,
Where my name in lights was billed,
But I am afraid these dreams,
Have been sadly unfulfilled.
However on the family front,
Could you really guess,
That my three children
Have helped me taste success?

So each in their own way,
Have stood out from the crowd,
Now with their own achievements,
They have made me proud,
My grandaughter, and six grandsons,
Travel the road of life,
Bringing so much happiness,
To myself, and my wife.

A R Tree

THE BRUNEL BRIDGE 1839

With a judder of brakes and a hissing of steam the Great Western train
  came to rest
Passengers and freight were transferred to the stage coach to continue
  their route to the west
The bridge on the river by Maidenhead town, where the Thames runs
  its easterly course
Was not built for strength, but just for the use of the yeoman with
  wagon and horse.

To mark the occasion in suitable style, when Victoria first came to reign
The worthy town burghers commissioned a new bridge, to herald the age
  of the train
The river officials decreed that the arch should be built to a meticulous
  plan
Made solely of brick with one central pier, a single continuous span.

The Doubting Thomas's threw up their hands, 'It will never stand' they
  did shout
'The design is too weak, it will crumble and fall, lives will be lost,
  there's no doubt'
'I will build you a bridge', said a young engineer, 'exactly as the
  plans state
It will bear the steam engines, and carriages too, will withstand
  whatsoever the weight.'

With a defiant whistle and a billow of steam, the brave iron horse
  chugged along
From Bucks o'er to Berks and on to the West, proving the pessimists
  wrong
A cheer for young Isambard Kingdom Brunel, let's give him a Hip, Hip,
  Hooray
Fifteen decades of safety, through five sceptred monarchs, and his
  bridge still stands proudly today.

Bridget Hole

TO THE VALLEY

The sun shines bright this winters day,
The air is crisp and dry,
The fog and mist have disappeared
And brightness fills the sky.

It's time now for my daily walk,
I stroll up Cutty's Lane,
Then into Bedwell Crescent
I find myself again.

I pass the telephone exchange,
Grotesque and towering high,
Above the Bedwell houses
That nestle closely by.

And opposite, St Andrews church,
My son was christened there,
But now it has no altar and
No sounds of holy prayer.

The shops and pub I quickly pass,
There is no time to dally,
I cannot get there soon enough
To see my lov'ly valley.

The same old route I go along,
It is the quickest way,
Just fifteen minutes and I'm there
For yet another day.

In summer and in winter time,
It's all the same to me,
Across the valley by the lakes
Is where I love to be.

F Collett

THE VENEERS OF BERKSHIRE

Oh come all ye
who want to see the world,
converge on Berkshire.
The jewel in Great Britain's crown
marvel at this special piece of land
we call our own.
Stroll along the river
or head into the hills,
it's a real life panacea
you'll have no need for pills.
It is easily connected
by the trains and motorways
this little piece of England
will always be the same.
So come all ye
and bring along your family and friends
spend some time in Berkshire.
I guarantee, you will not want to leave.

Raymond D Kelly

ROSE TINTED GLASSES

I watched the curtain rise, on another make believe tale,
Full of fun and laughter, or maybe dancing girls.
A heroine, a hero, the good men and the bad,
But rarely was there any trace of the kind of life we had.

I'd maybe cry a little, at a love match that went wrong,
But always end up singing, the show's most popular songs.
And it really never dawned on me, that life just wasn't like that,
Protected from reality, and all that it might lack.

I think what kept you going, was that somewhere inside of you,
There was still a tiny part, that truly believed it too.
Now that you're no longer here, I still go, once in a while,
And as the curtains open, I always wear a smile.

But very soon, that cherry grin, dissolves without a trace,
For nowadays the curtain hides no pain, and little grace.

The storylines reflect the truth, we suffer the hurt within,
And there are times that I'm grateful, that you're not here to
witness their sin.
And as the curtain closes, I want to remember what I saw,
Your enjoyment and contentment, through the rose-tinted glasses you wore.

Lynn Michelle Hiller

THE ORACLE OF NEWLANDS CORNER

He's been seen here on our North Downs heritage
Even when winter has been all in a rage.
A cyclist in woven garb you may have met
With similar-dressed fellows, they of the set
Of summertime lurkers who up on Newlands lie.
It's where pris'nors of Pan should all pause by and by.
And the coppered Oracle, his *Ponderous Grace*
Will be sunning his shanks not far from this place.
Weary of eye and shares in *Clear Skies Inc.*
- And a few others with similar link,
He, tired of vague resolve is waiting here yet
For Heaven-sent luminosity. To let
A slant from the sky, other than the sun
Show you and others how the world should run.

You may well have learned of something that binds us
To this earthly life. There's sometimes reminders
Of our special role in the order of things.
For, 'tis upon Saint Martha's a churchyard clings.
Amid darkened moss are tombstones leaning;
Makes me aware of the Oracle's meaning.
Grey tablets bearing unclear appellations
Of people now in other - worldly stations.

More light can be thrown on his strange look,
Seen *maybe now* in some rural nook.
On fragmented epitaph, worn by wind and rain,
Chosen One is seen. So is *Will Come Again.*

Richard B Callum

MY OLD WALTON

This Walton all my life, I have known,
From a small village, how it has grown,
Into quite a large, overcrowded town,
Buildings I knew, I sadly watched come down,

To be replaced by housing estates, all new,
Some so tall, that they spoilt the view,
Is this what they call progress,
Then it's not for me, I must confess,

Although the Thames, still gently flows,
Its banks with houses, also grows,
Will it remain, our one quiet spot,
With all these buildings, I fear not,

The best of times I've had, it seems,
When we had lanes, and many streams,
And horses walked, down every street,
And the air we breathed, was fresh and sweet,

And as a boy, could always roam,
Copses and woods, so close to home,
The ponds I fished, with rod and net,
This is the Walton, I cannot forget,

Enough of this, it has long since past,
Like most things in life, they never last,
But I feel sad, for the youngsters now,
Who cannot see the fields, with sheep and cow,

And smell the blossom, that hawthorns bring,
Each year, as we welcome in another Spring,
And hear the birds, that filled the air,
With songs, when we had hedgerows there,

I am always glad, I am of an age,
When countryside, was all the rage,
And was always safe, when out of sight,
Whether by day, or even at night.

Peter Brewer

LIVING IN BERKSHIRE

Stop all the traffic, block up the motorway
Prevent the cars from moving in the normal way
Silence the protesters and with cynical aplomb
Put up the road tax, make us pay a bomb

With aeroplanes circling, moaning overhead
Stacking in the skies for Heathrow or Stanstead,
Put cotton wool in the pink ears of sleeping youths
Let noisome pollution stay noiseless under roofs.

It is a curse, a bane, a blot and pest
My daily cross and week's unrest
At noon, at midnight, through talk and song
I fear that it might last forever. I wish I were wrong.

Our cars are not wanted now. Sell them off if you can.
Pack up your saloon. Dismantle the van.
Pour away the petrol, and sweep up the drive.
For nothing else will do to keep us all alive.

Richard Woolmer

MOVING PICTURES

Buckinghamshire leaves are green
But sometimes the wind is keen
It can chill your heart and blow away your dreams,
Whirling round towards the sky
Just to flutter down, and lie
Trampled, and forgotten, or so it seems.
The river tells a story
Of pictures on a screen
Remembered faces, and places far and near,
Though my dreams may come and go
There is something that I know,
I never found love anywhere but here,
No, I never found love anywhere but here.

Angie Von Tobel

ROADS

These long straight roads, she walks each day,
The trees, they watch, as if to say,
'Here comes the lass with weary feet,'
She'd like to rest, but where's the seat?
Before she trudges on with heavy bags,
So heavy, that her body sags.
Each day she tries a different road,
Keeps changing hands to ease her load.
She dreads the day the kids are with her,
She has no car, so that's no answer.
They hate the day of shopping's come,
'Please don't take us with you Mum,'
Moans and groans and 'I want a bun!'
Gone are the days, when shopping's fun.
So why on earth, when they built these roads,
Didn't someone think of her heavy loads?

Valerie Brown

MILTON KEYNES

I now live in Milton Keynes and before you jeer,
I will state emphatically, I love living here!
There are many facets to this town, more than you'd suppose,
Visitors see one or two and make judgement just on those.

You think of concrete cows and roundabouts every half a mile,
But we don't get traffic jams and the cows can raise a smile.
We've lots of open spaces, woods and parks and trees,
Many lakes and a grand canal, you can relax with ease.

There are several leisure centres and golf courses too,
A skating rink and cinemas, yes there's quite a lot to do.
There is ultra modern shopping if that is what you like,
And miles and miles of redways where you can walk or bike.

It isn't *all* new and modern, we have old places here,
Villages were incorporated, old pubs and tasty beer.
Houses still are being built, some estates look stark and new,
But they will settle and mature, in a year or two.

It isn't grey and dirty it's bright and very clean,
so suspend your judgement till all of it you've seen.
Milton Keynes has been the butt of jokes but you just wait and see,
We've a lot you'll envy, the last laugh will be with me.

Elizabeth Winn

MY HOME

Green fields, trees and space,
Hertfordshire is truly ace.
With greenbelt land and woods to see
Broxbourne is the place to be.

My childhood was spent there,
With no worries and lots of love to share.
People are friendly, helpful too,
and will always welcome you.

Broxbourne has lots to do,
a swimming pool and even a zoo.
Shops to visit and the River Lea
So much to fit in, you won't believe.

Carnivals in the summer time,
parks to walk and pubs to drink wine.
No night clubs here, people want peace,
but, beauty to see, the flowers and trees.

People come back when old,
as Broxbourne has that certain *hold.*
You want to come back, just to see,
that your childhood home, is still to be.

Tina Downham

SEASONS IN SURREY

Surrey, in Spring,
A beautiful sight,
Green fields all planted,
Trees, their buds about to burst
Bulbs of crocus and daffodil
Everywhere to be seen.

Surrey, in Summer,
Lovely tree lined lanes,
Smell of lilac and honeysuckle,
Fill the air and take your breath away,
Horses in the fields, cyclists too,
Picnics by the river, it's so gay.

Surrey, in Autumn
The leaves of trees now,
All browns and yellows,
Squirrels, running here and there,
Looking for nuts to store
Birds need feeding, eating all the berries.

Surrey, in Winter,
Looks quite bare; not much sign of life,
But there is still a beauty here,
The frost, makes the trees glisten,
Post vans, are now very busy,
As it's nearly Christmas, it snowed last night,
So we are now carpeted in white.

Linda J Proom

A NEW DAWN

Around the corner, the experience of dawn
my paradise lost - enlightened before me
morning dew transpires in the magical haze
that elusive thirst
that is the alchemy of the sun
as the valley road of lilley bottom
dwindles away in the foggy mist.

Amongst the summer fields of lost corn
The fall on an edge that begins to bite
the clouds of random will
in symbolic arrays
and through the trees
a twist of inner essence
that intuition with universal meaning.

The sunlight shines across the horizon
In a surf of glorious colour
to the ends of hidden doorways
so subtle in their depths
are the paths to the skyways of dawn

As my higher altitude descends
one final turn on my journey today
a glimpse of tomorrow stretches beyond
lower and lower
The tiles of the town come closer
on their way to work the faces look down
but I look up in the grasp of a new day
and I wonder . . .

George R Harrison

OUR HERTFORDSHIRE HERITAGE

Leafy lanes and fresh-green fields,
Village churches and country pubs,
Houses big and houses small
Diversity abounds.

Meandering rivers and babbling brooks,
Commons teaming with wildlife,
People rushing in their cars,
No time to look around.

Cathedrals and stately homes,
Gardens and parks to explore,
The beauty of nature all around,
But London's just next door.

Sport to suit both young and old
Lots to do and see
History and a sense of the past
So proud we should be.

We've had St. Alban and George Bernard Shaw
Very famous men
Kings, Queens, Lords and Dukes
And politicians too.

Young people with a sense of purpose
Well educated and full of life
The future lies with them
The present with us.

Hertfordshire has it all
A lovely place to live
But too many cars, too little time
To appreciate all that we have.

Sheila Cochrane

USED TO

We used to walk for miles
Across the fields and stiles
In my younger day,
Now everyone owns a car,
You can't go very far
Before meeting a motorway.

There used to be friendly faces
And lots of open spaces
Where the children could play,
Now every street and stranger
Represents a danger
They're not allowed to stray.

There used to be little shops,
We had to make many stops
For butcher, grocer, baker,
Now there's a Megastore
That sells both less and more
And occupies an acre.

Still, we're better off by far,
We own a house and car,
We really can't complain.
Besides, it's much too late,
They've built a big estate
On top of Memory Lane.

Peter Williams

SANDRIDGE SUNDAY

It is Sunday in Sandridge.
The rising, falling, bells across the fields
Call the faithful to renew their lives,
Joining in with the sounds of Sunday death
As fur and feather flee fast
From the life-deprivers.

Cars sit quietly outside voice-bulging inns;
Sit silent in the summer heat
Like tethered horses,
Patient in the waiting.

A shepherds crook stands in the corner
Of the stone-floored room,
Now cold as the hand of its user past,
Who lies beneath Sandridge soil

Two gummed men sit in the dug-out bus shelter
Observing ear-ringed youths passing by.
They look and wonder
Through great war eyes.

In a brown study, the vicar sits
Listening to the transient ones passing through;
Mourning yet another who has passed on,
Chunk chunk - sounds the pick on solid Sandridge soil.

Village of my father,
And his father,
His father,
His . . .

James Byron-Archer

MY VILLAGE

Now I'm old I sit and dream,
Of a village by a cool clear stream.
A spot that was my boyhood home,
Weathampstead named in William's tome.

Then the Lea was crystal clear,
I walked its banks without a care.
From ancient mill to Marford Old,
Through meads of King Cups shining gold.

Off times when wandering all alone,
Through the Belgic Dyke I'd roam.
Coleman Green I'd sometimes reach.
There the Tinker once did preach.

By Amwell's Lane to where Down Green,
Overlooks the village scene.
Down Brewhouse Hill to old flint school,
Where I learnt life's golden rule.

St. Helens broach spire, tall,
In regal state towers over all.
Many rural crafts were seen,
In the street twixt *Swan* and stream.

Farrier and smith with forges bright,
Tailor, saddler, and wheelwright.
Past the miller grinding corn,
To *Rose Lane* where I was born.

Now wherever I may chance to roam,
Or whatever place I call my home.
My pensive thoughts do often flee,
To *Wathamstede* astride the Lea.

S G Dollimore

ON THE BACK EIGHT AT THE ABBEY

The dark, velvet handling of the treble,
How deep, and sweet, and soft an envelopment
In music, history, architecture
And time

When the bells
Go round
Near perfectly struck,
Rhythmic
And timeless

The flow of warmth and joy
In the working together
Of the ringers and the bells
On the back eight
When the bells go
On their appointed courses
Till the end.

Gracie Fitzsimmons

THE MAN WHO FELL IN LOVE WITH A FIELD

Happy the man who husbands you, who ploughs your bare flanks,
Who waits with you in the waiting months and watches
For the first - trick of light or true - show of life.
He will know spontaneous gratitude, giving of thanks
For the melting line of winter hills, for swatches
Of windblown velvets, for such a dowry from such a wife.

Cover the pheasant, hide the muntjak, feed the mouse,
Calm the hare's terror, bid the poppy to your bed,
Console sad thinkers, mend breaking hearts,
Endure man's bookish, fumbling intercourse.
You are the England we lie back and think of, thread
Tied of our fathers, thread which never parts.

Tony Brignull

SWEET HERTFORDSHIRE

In Hertfordshire, in Hertfordshire
At last I've come to rest
Having travelled all the world
Sweet Hertfordshire is best

I've sometimes been to Chipperfield
Where cricket on the green
Once featured in a special film
No longer to be seen . . .

From there on to the Gaddesdens
Or down to Aldbury . . .
That wondrous part of Hertfordshire
Is ever dear to me

Then eastwards through Saint Albans
Through Hatfield, Hertford, Ware,
To dear old Bishop's Stortford
My soul was nurtured there

But Harpenden, dear Harpenden
The village of my birth
The place I still remember
As the sweetest place on earth

Church Green, though changed, is much the same
As the Church, where once I prayed
And on the Common still I find
Good country cricket played

But where has gone the Silver Cup
Beneath the Baa-Lamb Trees?
They told me it had been filled up
Because it bred disease.

Oh! Sweet and lovely county
My wondrous Hertfordshire
I thank you for your bounty
Forever you are dear.

Maxwell Bruce

OUR SHIRE

Leafy Hertfordshire is the well known theme,
Varied fields and trees are many to be seen.
Enhanced by the seasons as the colours unfold,
Crops in the fields next to sheep in the fold.

Picturesque villages unchanged by the time,
Still nestle where copses and woodland abound.
Estates now mushroom round sprawling towns,
As motorways cut through rural surrounds.

Office blocks tower so tall and erect,
Unseen folk work inside at their desk.
Shops in the town brim with goods for purchase,
And out of town shopping so much on the increase.

Historic houses and churches are still all around,
Majestic and beautiful, they are to be found.
Market towns survive for us to ponder and browse,
What a wealth of ancient and modern, this Hertfordshire of ours.

Dorothy Garvan

THE DECLINE OF A ONCE PROUD TOWN

More than forty years have gone
Since to Harpenden first I came
The gas lights flickered eerily
As I stepped down from the train.

And though it was quite late that night
The last train down the line
To show me where I had to go
A stranger took the time

A small and pleasant rural town
It was, back in those days
But now the changes have been rung
In oh so many ways.

There were the civic leaders then,
To make the people proud
Men like *Bond* and *Gingell*
Who stood out from the crowd.

The cinemas have long since gone
The market hall demolished
Harridens store we'll see no more
And the butchers have all been abolished.

The verges are all left uncut
The streets with litter strewn
The pavements crumble 'neath our feet
The town has gone to ruin.

But though it's going downhill fast
Not all is doom and gloom,
Let's get back to autonomy
Then the town again can boom.

A H Richardson

OXHEY VILLAGE

My surroundings have changed so much,
Since growing up here
Once with space to touch,
Now ones car must be near!

Everywhere you look are cars
More new roads engulf us
Like prisoners have bars
We have more and more cars!

The fields and woods so near to see
The beauty for all to enjoy
If only we could walk free
No traffic, no noise, only joy.

Revelling in the wonderful scenery
For a time you can feel calm
Walking through the beautiful greenery
Away from man's harm.

Watching the horses roaming around
How lucky we are to have all this
Please do not touch this sacred ground
Feel it, smell it, it's pure bliss.

Why must man build and destroy?
Make way, make way,
Man must have his little toy!
We can not have our say.

When I am old
And long in the tooth
Will it all be gone?
The youth must know the truth
Not, I hope in a song!

Sharon Foxhall

UNTITLED

A wealth of treasures beyond compare
await all who venture there
fields of green with golden corn
glisten in the sun as day is born
spring flowers bursting through the earth
bring colour, joy and mirth

our waterways at this time of year
are full of wildfowls' offspring, who
delight their visitors, young and old,
tiny creatures - a fluff of gold
they bob along under mother's eye
sampling the offerings of you and I
such precious sights, though common to see
reflect the essence of Hertfordshire to me

from bustling Barnet to sleepy Ware
historical sites are scattered wide
across our beautiful countryside
from civilised Romans to ancient tribes
painters, poets and notable scribes
have all left their mark upon the land
preserving it is in our hand

museums hold the key
to how life used to be
country houses are more up to date
with concerts, fairs and country fetes

and as the sun goes down
life springs forth within our towns
pubs and clubs, theatres too
there is an abundance of things to do
those of us who live within this shire
should take time to see and admire
the glory of this pleasant land

Linda Jameson

THE HERTFORDSHIRE VILLAGE OF LEAVESDEN

The blacksmiths irons were in the fire, bellows blowing
making flames jump higher.
Watching the cobbler working at his last, tapping nails
in leather shoes so fast.
The village school with two small classes, the playground
full of happy lads and lasses.
A post office, that sold penny sweets and fizzy pop, and was
also known, as the gossip shop.
Small neat cottages, standing in a row, with blazing coal fires,
that made faces glow.
Gas lamps flickering in the night, giving out shadowy dancing lights.
A red brick chapel stood so proud, where children sang their
hymns out loud.
In fields and woods we did run free, and had toast with dripping
for our tea.
Now village life was rather hard, the cold water tap and toilet.
Was down at the bottom of the yard.
Now with the march of progress, our village life has died.
No fields or woods remaining, instead houses stand side by side.
I feel sorry for the children, the country side has gone.
I am thankful for my memories, of a village life that's gone.
Such very happy memories, that go on and on and on.

Sylvia Lintern Fahey

NATURE IN THE NEW TOWN
STEVENAGE 1992

Shelled skeletons green again on the concrete verge
Reclothing thin tramps with luxuriant foliage.

Stones stacked at the top of the artificial pool
Pour silver honey down a sonorous waterfall.

Duck brown as mudpies chug ahead of their serpentine wake.
The boatclub clangs with echoes of a coastal shipwreck.

Gardens groom themselves below windows where babies cry
Bell-loud with hunger or worse. Bedrooms snore or sigh,

Tenanted by common dreams. Seagulls cruise the summery air
Counterpointing brittle butterflies see-sawing everywhere

As the wind screws the dancing trees. The sun seems a Bethlehem star
This afternoon of stunning heat. Waves of flowers are

Swept wild around the shores of the bumblebee's flightpaths.
Teenagers tumble with one another, giving each other baths

In the wider lake of love. We follow on where children play
On swings and roundabouts. The dogs each have their day

By the resonant water. A girl cartwheels, her legs scissoring the sky's sheet
Where the light is dying with premature harvest of gold wheat

Cropped on the hanging horizon. The evening traffic roars
Home to East Enders as the tigerish tabby claws

A songbird to early death. The last shoppers bus back,
Loaded up like pirates. Winter has suffered its last heart attack

Spring is skipping ahead and summer's almost arrived.
We bask like rescued seals so glad to be still alive.

Roland Gurney

HARPENDEN

I know a very pleasant town
Where the grassy banks abound,
Busy shops with tree lined streets
Restaurants, cafes, special treats
Churches, schools and open spaces
Parks and many other places.

I like to watch the trains run high
As if they're riding through the sky
Winding through the trees at night
With their dashing, brilliant light
Carrying passengers on their way
Home from work or off to play.

There's golf and cricket on the green
Which helps to make a pleasant scene.
Houses which are trim and neat,
Gardens where the flowers are sweet.
A centre for the old and young
Yes, Harpenden's a lot of fun.

Vanda Gilbert

WHEN THE LANE WAS A LANE

Three generations in a waiting room
Many years between departure from the womb
A baby, a mother and a stately man
Who smiled at the baby through an ageing tan

The mother listened as the old man spoke
Of days gone by and of elderly folk
He began to recall the way things used to be
Painting a picture for the mother to see

When the lane was a lane, he started to say
And there weren't many houses along this way
And the only sound to be heard in the day
Was the singing of birds so pretty and gay

And the only smell was either fruity and sweet
Or the hay in the fields or harvested wheat
And the length of the lane was measured in feet
As we walked to the village in the summers heat

He continued to tell the tale of his life
Of the fifty five years in his house with his wife
Of the fields that were now full of houses in rows
As you walked for miles following the crows

Although Bushey Village has changed in many parts
It has kept the essential beauty of Herts
The green of the fields can still be seen in the view
And the birds are still singing with the sweet morning dew

His eyes glazed and warm came back from the past
His memories were long and his experience vast
The mother bounced the baby up and down on her knee
When the baby was old what would her memories be?

Julia Holt

CHURCH END

In between the pub front door and workhouse,
the narrow street, that leads on to the church,
and windows, either side reflect each other
like some old scroll or ancient document
reflecting images of life, of past and present
complete, with dated writing on a wall,
When someone notched the time of day in history
that, no doubt will be read by those to come.

Meanwhile though, the peacefulness of silence
is pregnant in the stillnesses of air,
that wrap around the buildings to envelop
the echoing of church bells everywhere,
and bring the mind, to wander down the ages,
and search around, for remnants of the past,
perhaps, to glimpse, a long gone face, at windows
in atmospheres, of long ago, that last.

Walter Gilder

HERTFORDSHIRE

Hertfordshire's the place to be,
Badgers foxes and deer run free,
Winding lanes encased in trees,
Fields of corn flutter in the breeze.
Carpets of bluebells in the wood sway,
While blackbird, robin and blue tits have their say.
Rivers full of fish galore,
Country walks for all to explore,
Our county town was once so quaint,
They've pulled it about so now it ain't,
So if you want to forget your ills,
Breeze away into the hills,
To soak up all the atmosphere
Of our romantic Hertfordshire.

E Hankin

WELL IN WELWYN

We're always
Well in Welwyn
'Cos Welwyn
Suits us well!
We live inside
A little house
One with
No doorbell!
It contains
Our nest egg too
Nice and easy
Soon to sell!
So that we may
Then vacate!
Buy a small
Country estate!

Catherine B Parness

THE RIVER STORT

A river runs through the middle of our town
As it does, through the middle of our name
It brought prosperity to us years ago
And it also brought us fame.

If I mention the name Dick Whittington
You'd think of him and his cat
But you'd be very wrong my friend
Because it didn't mean just that.

The cat in question, was in fact a boat
With which Dick plied his trade
He used the river continuously
That's how his fortune was made.

Bringing coal and timber down from London
And taking back meat and grain
The journeys took several days you know
But he did it come sunshine snow or rain.

Eventually he became Lord Mayor of London
Wearing his cap and red gown
All because of the trade that was there
Between Bishops Stortford and old London town

Now things have changed a lot since then
But the river is still the same
Lush green meadows used to border it
Then the builders came.

Concrete buildings, Erected on either side
Where the fish swim, there are shopping trolleys
It's amazing how man can change in time
And introduce such follies.

Tony Knight

THE PLANNERS ERRORS - RURAL BLIGHT

Roselands *Hoddesdon* is where we live.
We chose it from the rest.
But now the local planners
are reducing it, to less than second best.

'Roselands is the unspoilt place
that we will build on next.
No matter that the residents
will all be sorely vexed.'

'No matter that the wildlife,
that on that green belt thrive,
will have to move away from there
to let the lodgers drive.'

'No matter that the noise and smells
will upset every local.
Us council planning officers
will not be at all vocal.'

'We need the houses there, you see,
forget we knock down others.
It upsets far more residents
their wives, their kids, their mothers.'

They would not build these houses
where they have made *their* home.
They'd rather build them on the fields
where fox and dear and rabbit roam.

They know *they've* made an error
but will *they* put it right?
No. *They'd* rather keep their silence
and leave us with rural blight.

Denis Bindoff

BLINDMAN'S LANE

Blindman's Lane is neither blind nor a lane.
It sees all things and nothing stays the same.
Tottering ladies with large bulging tummies,
Soon to be non-stop fussing new mummies.
turn into
Teeny babies in pristine pastel prams,
staring skywards at jiggling fluffy lambs
turn into
Mouthy toddlers who given half a chance,
Will lead their mothers a very merry dance.
turn into
Bright eyed nursery school girls and boys,
Full of action and bucketfuls of noise.
turn into
Infant pupils - big school at last,
All thoughts of babyhood now well past.
turn into
Junior school people who know it all,
As heavy as mum now and nearly as tall.
But soon it is time to say your goodbyes,
With a lump in your throat and tears in your eyes,
turn for the last time and never again
farewell and our love go to Blindman's Lane.

Patricia Lloyd

SAWBRIDGEWORTH
'THE SETTLEMENT BESIDE THE BRIDGE MADE OF WITHIES'

Being a Northerner, I feel I can give a clear view,
Of a Southern life which I've become accustomed to.
When I moved to Hertfordshire, I knew from the first day,
At last I'd found an abode where I wanted to stay.

On moving from a small seaside resort,
To a town called Sawbridgeworth, has certainly taught
Me, how different the people, lifestyle, and surroundings can be,
Even though only a short distance from my home by the sea.

Nestling in some of the prettiest Hertfordshire countryside,
A thriving town, known far and wide,
Yet despite its growth, the charm remains,
Once visited, the memories, you'll always retain.

The locals tell me this is an historical town,
Picturesque, peaceful and inviting I have found.
Portraying a pleasant village atmosphere,
Whether a visitor or resident you'll feel welcome here.

If you close your eyes and imagine a place,
Of harmonious people, young, old and of mixed race.
What would you picture? What would you see?
What would your ideal place be?

I have found the picture, I've been looking for,
No need for searching anymore.
Wherever you go, and whatever you do,
I hope you find your paradise too.

Rachel Farr

HERTFORDSHIRE

Welwyn Garden City
Is the place to be
Beauty all around
For all of us to see
We have a county library
Roller city too
Also a barn theatre
Where they perform for you.
It's such a lovely town
Greenery and trees
All planted with care
Residents to please.
Boating lake at Standborough
Outdoor swimming too
Golfing courses giving choice
Of those we have two.
Play on King George playing fields
With your bat and ball
If you would like a meal
Then book at bushy hall.
Take a ride to Hatfield House
Residence for Queens
Deer roam free in Brocket Park
With permission from the Lord
Welwyn Garden's great
That's why it's home to me
Don't forget the countryside
It's here for all to see.

Marjorie Ann Warden

HERTFORD - MY COUNTY TOWN

I live fairly close to Hertford North station
Where people arrive from every nation.
I wonder what strangers first think of our town
As from the raised platform they hurry down.

'How rural,' some say, as they look over fields
And a view of cows and swans is revealed.
'A county town - oh surely not,
An overgrown village is what we've got!'

Turn to the left, or go straight across,
If it's shops you seek, you'll see the loss.
There were corner shops in every street,
But now these are dwellings with curtains so neat.

Turn to the right and your views will change
As over town houses and flats your eyes range.
Past the hospital, imposing and old
But where locals are cared for by hearts of gold.

On past the church in St Andrew Street
Where shops full of antiques with each other compete;
Now we're almost in centre of town,
Library, river and castle of county renown.

In the centre of town a street market you'll find
On Saturday, streets full of shoppers lined.
Bargains galore in greengrocery, books,
Plants, fish and cheese, jewellery fine if one looks.

Pubs, cafes, craft shops, department store too,
Newsagents, kitchenware and models to view.
The Shire Hall, refurbished demands our attention,
The old Corn Exchange deserves more than a mention.

I'm proud to live in our county town,
In a quiet little spot where contentment I own.

Liz Campbell

WELWYN GARDEN CITY IN THE RAIN

This uniform and quiet place,
Caught in the pounding, blanching rain,
Has lost itself, seems all the same,
Appears to hold a neutral face.

As red brick changes to damp clay,
The little windows watch like eyes,
Drip with water. They surely cry!
Shop fronts shudder in the grey.

A garden city needs the sun,
Longs for the warmth, the light of spring
Needs the detail that season brings,
Yearns for winter over and done.

Dull figures dressed in brown and blue,
Hurry quickly down Howardsgate.
They cross the road, forget to wait
and look - as cold, grey people do.

A starling darts around the lawn,
the privet hedge, the neat pruned tree.
He looks for food but he is free.
Unlike people he does not mourn.

He knows that spring will come again,
Will bring the city's colour home,
From where it hides when winter roams.
He'll wait and look, forget the rain.

As the burst fades to a shower,
From Wigmores North I see her run,
Rainbow brolley, mac like the sun,
A laughing little girl; a flower.

E A Verlander

ENCHANTED CHILDHOOD

Inside the pocket of a Hertfordshire town
where like a giant hand the houses span.
The River Stort like a fairy-tale ran,
like some frisking white magic of Peter Pan.
Remember, sparkles of sunlight on the Stort's small fall,
rushing through toes and nets when we were small.
The same sunlight raining onto the distant wood,
the trees, the park, the red-bricked cornershop,
these sun-drenched places where once we stood.
One can still see,
through the dusty pattern
on a Rye Street window pane,
how the memory of childhood stains.
The fields green and sometimes brown
like a silk scarf pulled round the town.
Barrells Down always stretched far behind
Galloways Road and any crime.
One remembers,
the metal rail on the pathway's edge,
the barking dog and the trailing hedge.
The slope that ran up high and narrow,
where silver fell in the whirr of sparrow.
Strange, how a hill can become a ladder to the sky,
Glitter the moments of childhood,
these moments do not die.

J A Lawrence

CROOKHAMS, WELWYN GARDEN CITY, HERTFORDSHIRE

I see an Anglo-Saxon countryside,
Where pigs, sheep, bears and wolves abide,
And a hamlet nestling there.
The homes protected from wolves and bear.

In a field near a babbling brook,
I see a shepherd with his crook,
Gathering his sheep into their fold,
Where they can shelter from the cold.

I see some Anglo-Saxon wives,
Busily getting on with their lives.
Gathering fallen branches in nearby wood.
Their children helping as children should.

While others are collecting sheeps' wool caught on briars.
Coming towards them are three friars,
Who are travelling to a new monastic home.
Obeying an order from the Pope in Rome.

I now see coming into view,
A family, with a pig or two,
Who are looking for somewhere to make their home,
As they wish to settle, and no more roam.

It seems they are welcomed here,
And need not move on as was their fear.
This is the Crookhams that I can see.
This is my street's history.

D Leete

THE HERTS OF THE MATTER

It ain't no Middlesex, Essex or Lancs
When it comes to cricket, it's a big no thanks
In football it's Watford and not much more
If it's talent you want, you know the score

The lakes or Scotland is the place to be
For a spot of fellwalking or a chance to ski
Herts, on the other hand, is flatter than toast
Miles from mountains, even further from coast

A farm's not a farm without its pigs,
Its sheep, its cows, its thingamajigs
But the fields in Herts are full of grarse,
Wheat and corn, it's such a farce

An accent is a funny thing
Going undetected when you sing
But when you talk it makes me larff
And I'll cringe behind my Liverpool scarf

Who am I to pen this verse?
Living elsewhere could be worse
There's education, no doubt the best
It's in young people that Herts invest

So what has Hertfordshire county got
In fairness, I suppose, it's quite a lot
Old towns, new towns, the first garden city
And historic houses to conclude this ditty.

Roger A Inglis

BUCKS LIFE

When I close my eyes and think of Bucks,
I see those village ponds with their ducks
And the running bourne with water clear
And darting trout when they feel you near.

The old church with its flinted wall
And nearby beech which stands so tall.
The filtered light on leaves below
Where for a short time the bluebells glow.

The soft green hills in sun or rain
Or the golden field with ripening grain
The lonely tractor passing through
And the hedgerows hiding fox and shrew.

On top of the hills the cold winds blow
And as you look down it helps you know
What beauty it is - How blest are we,
That live here now and have eyes to see.

These are the things I always will
See when I dream of the Chiltern Hill.
And as time goes by and changes come
We must keep it safe for daughter 'n' son.

Michael Rush

A TASTE OF SURREY

The Black Prince at Farnham our very first venue
Trouble was the great choice on the menu,
Pints of lager or medium white wine,
Six of each, yes, that'll be fine.
On to the Alma where the drinks flow,
Never tried a snowball, let's have a go,
Martinis, cinzanos, bacardis and coke,
Lively and friendly us Surrey folk.
Four miles to Tilford to the Barley Mow
And here we found ten more people in tow.
Woolpack at Elstead we drank pernod and black,
But by then we felt ready to hit the sack.
Oh don't bottle out, the night is still young,
The King's Arms at Blackwater for another one,
Here for good measure we'll try rum and pep,
Or maybe we won't, don't let's lose our step.
Home to Farnham in our mini van,
We've got a chauffeur, so indulge in a can.
Last port of call the Spotted Cow
Quickly, last orders we must choose now,
Twenty five glasses and mineral water
Nicely served by the Landlord's daughter.
Let's finish the night in true Surrey style
Down the road for a curry, it's only a mile!

Julie Collins

WEYBRIDGE WOMEN

Weybridge women never linger,
Do not seem to want to chat.
Seldom ever lift a finger,
Want to be where the action's at.
Baskets filled to the brim,
Expensive, calorie-counted foods
to keep them slim.
They do not look at prices of the
food they buy.
But pick up trifles that catch the eye.
Oh such studied elegance in their colourful
Designer tracks.
Shiny hair, long, lacquered nails,
The hard work all this entails.
The Limos, the furs, the house on the hill,
No children's laughter, they're away at school,
So many empty hours, time to kill.
Mirrored behind all this facade I see,
Some very lonely women looking back at me.

Kathleen Gates

THIS COUNTRY LIFE IN BUCKINGHAMSHIRE

Far from the bustling crowds
on hills that ramble wide
I climb towards each looming scarp
to view the countryside.
Here a special peace I find
my feet may wander free
There is no better place on earth
that I would rather be.

Under the Beechwood tree to rest
amongst the primrose and the pine
with humble memories of yesterday
filling empty corners of my mind.
To smell the scent of flowers that grow
secluded by the Icknield Way
In hidden woodlands scattered far
where once I used to run and play.

The Cuckoo singing heralds spring
my heart is lighter than before.
Would that I could stay here with my thoughts
to keep her tune forever more.
To sit in shady dells of sweetness
reminding me of childhood days
or crunching leaves beneath my feet
while others seldom stop to gaze.

I recall those moments spent in freedom
with sunlight shining on my face
as with childish eyes I played
in peaceful innocence and grace.
This corner, this patch of pastures green
is to me a thing of strong desire.
This is my love, my home, my all
this country life in Buckinghamshire.

Susan Lacey

THE BUCKINGHAMSHIRE SCENE

Woodland glades and leafy shades
Have endured here, for decades,
In our county of historic fame,
Where the beechwoods autumnal flame
Beckon visitors by the score,
Charming all since time immemorial
At Burnham Beeches, an open door
Depicting scenes serene, pictorial.

Captain's Wood, its trees so rare,
Based on chalklands, from *Dorset fair*,
Both young and old long enchants
With waving fronds of bluebell plants,
And farmland vistas below, in a vale,
Where Chesham farmers have toiled for years
And woodland travellers followed a trail
Carved through scrub and bracken, it onward veers.

Where beechwood forests long prevail
In dense, green places of Aylesbury Vale,
Find mossy banks, coppice and glade
By master craftsmen long purveyed
To cottages of brick and flint
And manor-houses of great renown,
Their skills turned wood to subtle tint,
Adorning many a Saxon town
And Norman churches, in sleepy villages
With endearingly enchanting names,
Ancient barns for yeoman-farmers built
In medieval times; for men of fame
Who hailed from this shire, arms a-tilt,
To add to England's burning flame.

Julia Eva Yeardye

HAVE YOU BEEN TO WOKING, FRIEND?

Have you been to Woking, friend?
Have you been to Woking?
Mad planners' changes never end and no, friend, I'm not joking.
Even Rome ignored the place - no Roman roads you see,
But Saxons came and Vikings came tho' why's a mystery.
The planners' concrete covers all and hides our history.
Have you been to Woking friend?
Really *been* to Woking?
The trains are good, I'll give you that,
But the rest of Woking's rather flat.
One hundred and fifty years of rail,
And fifty years of planners.
If only they would go away,
We'd all put out the banners!
When Henry VIII was just a lad,
He hunted in his granny's pad called Woking
His daughter Elizabeth the first
Most surely thought it was the worst-place she'd ever seen,
And even tho' she was the Queen,
She said goodbye to Woking.
Have you been to Woking friend?
Have you been to Woking?

Doris W Withers

THE DIRT AND DUST OF EPSOM

I step outside of my oak front door.
And feel the force of the autumn breeze,
I take in a breath of the whispery air,
And as I do I loudly sneeze.

The fumes of the cars, the smoke is intense,
I lean against the neighbour's fence.
My lungs will collapse, my heart will stop,
Soon I'm going to blow my top.

My chest feels sore and full of smoke,
I keep on walking but really slow,
I cannot breathe, I feel so sick,
How we all live, I do not know.

The fumes of the cars, the smoke is intense,
I lean against the neighbour's fence,
My lungs will collapse, my heart will stop,
Soon I'm going to blow my top.

I turn the corner and can smell tar,
Drilling is near, with dust and smoke,
More pollution made by these machines,
One of these days I swear I'll choke.

The fumes of the cars, the smoke is intense,
I lean against the neighbour's fence,
My lungs will collapse, my heart will stop,
Soon I'm going to blow my top.

Jenny Orr (13)

RURAL LAMENT

As hedges and the trees are stripped away,
The farmland sprawls across in dusty leas
Along the verge of that new motorway.

The butterflies might die as farmers spray
Their crops with toxic mists to halt disease,
As hedges and the trees are stripped away.

The flint-stone barns are falling in decay,
While barn owls move their homes like refugees
Along the verge of that new motorway.

In Margery Wood the stricken bluebells may
Renew their magic carpet for the bees,
As hedges and the trees are stripped away.

Yet wild wings could survive the cull, to prey
A safe environment, and breed with ease
Along the verge of that new motorway.

But windmills' fettered sails are *on display*
And prairie landscapes future artists tease,
As hedges and the trees are stripped away
Along the verge of that new motorway.

Pam Clarke

MISSENDEN SUMMER SCHOOL

Embroiderers sketchbook - pictures in silk and wool
Varied colours at Missenden school
Bucks landscape in pastel - water-colour - oils.
Portrait painting - colour images - Heirloom dolls.

Chinese brushwork a delicate art.
Chinese Health studies - a different start.
Upholstery repaired - Jewellery gleaming,
Talking with confidence - character beaming.

Figures taking shape in plaster and wood.
Video pictures - hold it - that's good.
Antiques - a study so vast
Beautiful things out of the past.

Poetry, crossed out - discussed - now re-write.
Spirit of music from darkness to light.
Lacquer - pigments in resin suspended.
Seeds sown this week - sorry it's ended.

Mollie Maclerie

THE BEAUTIFUL BEECH

Echoing the forward chestnut
The woodland beech has changed her dress
For the late summer ball.

She wears a golden collar
Above her gown of green
With feathery fronds around her head,
The prettiest ever seen.

But soon she'll change her dress again
For a copper-coloured sheath,
A glorious, glowing challenge
A carpet of flame beneath.

In defiance of dark days,
Her beauty will stay in the mind
Through November frost and fog
It will warm the heart and eye,

Until spring comes again
Under a clear blue sky.

Deirdre White

POETRY

This paper used to be a tree -
It didn't need words to tell a story.
It stood.

Silent, but not depressive.
Tall, but not oppressive.
Strong, but not aggressive.

You can learn a lot from trees.

Lovers have the bans read out to congregations
But on its bark they carve their loving declarations.

Now the wood's been turned to paper.
It's blank again.
It needs a poet
To interpret,
And make it
Poetree.

Graham Barrie Langley

THE FINAL ACT . . .

November thirty-nine, and with a great deal of pride,
Farnham's theatre began
With Bernard Shaw and Oscar Wilde.
Throughout three decades to follow
It continued to grow;
Local people of all ages
Supporting each show.

With standing room only we launched an appeal
to restore Brightwells House,
A building ideal
for creating a cultural space
Combining the qualities of progress and grace.

Michael Redgrave agreed to lend us his name,
And in May seventy-four the new stage became
Fair Verona, with Will's Lovers the choice;
Farnham theatre-goers had cause to rejoice.

For the next twenty years our Redgrave found fame
Bringing laughter and tears in the fantasy game.
Something for all, a *cavalcade* of delight,
But recessional problems made the future less bright.

Now our Redgrave is dark, the curtain's come down,
A sorry and painful blow for the town.
But the people are determined,
We must bring it back.
For ourselves, for our children
It *cannot* stay black.

Phyllida Adams

HERTFORDSHIRE

Hertfordshire has been my home
Never had the urge to roam.
Bedfordshire lies to the North
Where the Chiltern Hills come forth.
To the South is London town
(Commuters going up and down).
No mountain peaks or even lakes,
No tourist spots, nor what it takes.
Two garden cities do we host
Letchworth, Welwyn, we must boast.
Lovely trees line every street
Looking oh so trim and neat!
Motorways run up and down,
From the North to London town.
High speed trains go rattling by
What a noise and how they fly!
Towns there are where we can shop,
Airports handy for that hop.
St Albans Abbey stands on high
The Martyr's bones are buried nigh.
Hatfield House where good Queen Bess
Spent her childhood, more or less.
Watford is the largest town,
Oh! so busy, makes us frown.
Best of all are pastures green
Where there is a rural scene.
Village greens with duckponds nigh
Houses thatched, which catch the eye.
Commuter belt it may well be
But Hertfordshire is home to me.

Brenda Dawson

NEVER

Have you ever sat and wondered what life would be like
Without a bit of countryside to walk on or ride a bike.
Never seeing grass again or trees with leaves so green.
Never seeing frost come down and covering them with a sheen.
No wildlife just wondering free.
No birds chirping or singing from their trees.
Never waiting for the spring to come.
Never seeing flowers opening up to the sun.
Or leaves changing colours in the autumn glow.
And everything covered by the winter snow.
Never experiencing country life and lots of fresh air.
That means never knowing the real Buckinghamshire.

Mandy Penn

A WELCOME

There's a little place in Stortford
Where the unemployed can go
They can have a game of dominoes
Or have a dart to throw

You can play a game of billiards
And enjoy a game for free
If you want to enjoy it more
You can buy a coffee or tea

You will find the tea and coffee
And sandwiches all half price
The ones that serve behind the bar
You will find them very nice

When you have enjoyed your stay
And it's time for you to leave
You are welcome to come back any time
Don't stay at home and grieve.

Bert Booley

IN SHELTER

Now residing two storeys high
I see the sky
With downy clouds
And planes vapours trailing
when the skies are blue.
Many birds - will they now fly
to other lands as our winter approaches?
            Another World is opened to me
As before I lived in a house in the country.
            Here I view
            Vans, coaches, cyclists
            Pedestrians - dog walkers
            Cars which stop
            To visit the shop.
And sounds - so many varied sounds
            Sirens - Ambulance.
            Sirens - Police.
            Sirens - Fire.
Music from stationary cars -
a bubbly laugh from a child passing by.
And the wind, when wild
Sways the distant trees.
Then the golden sun, whose rays
Brighten my room, and make joyous days.

F Lanceley Heaton

SURREY

If you ever come to Surrey
Please don't leave us in a hurry
Take a little time to ponder
Where you'd like to walk and wander.

There's quite a lot to see
If you care to come with me
You can go up into town
See the shops and look around.

But for a really special treat
You must leave the busy street
Come and look behind the scenes
To see the wildlife that can be seen.

Then at dusk the fox will out
Hear the local children shout
He went right past us in a rush
We know it's him we saw his brush.

A tree above the fox's den
Is home to Magpie, Robin, Wren
There are many different kinds
Just for you to come and find.

A squirrels home is his drey
And hedgehogs slowly pass your way
Wild rabbits in the fields
Waiting for the farmers yield.

So if you chance along this way
On a lovely summer's day
Take some time to stop and stare
Of local beauty everywhere.

Susan Caile

THE WAY THROUGH HERTFORDSHIRE

The Gt. North Road of long ago
Out of London through Hertfordshire
Then coach and horse, the pace so slow
A dusty track, otherwise a mire.

Be it shank's pony, the only other way
For the likes of you and me
An inn for the thirsty and a place to stay
The very poor, a hedgerow shelter, the stars to see

Country town with cobbled street
Footsore weary, a begging bowl
Rarely a friend that you would meet
Hard times indeed for the troubled soul

Baldock town to Templar fame
Thirty seven miles from London, they say
Through to the North the traveller came
In olden times, the long travelling day

Now speeds the coach and car to the North
No footsore traveller these modern times
Lightly clad, from a vehicle they step forth
For refreshment they look for the signs

How times have changed with the passing years
Now who can foresee the way ahead
There are those around with many fears
Too many vehicles, congested roads, a future of dread.

Robin Barker

FROM COOMBE HILL

County of beech woods, chalk and clay,
Where, acorn-marked, the Chiltern Way
Wends through a paradise of green
By pastures, crops and woodland scene,

There, gold furze, rabbits, wind-tossed kites
Adorn the downy Coombe Hill heights,
While, tranquil in the copse below,
Half-hidden, the roofs of Chequers show.

Through chalk and scrub the track winds down
To farms and fields and Aylesbury town,
Whose church tower scans with eye serene
The patchwork Vale that lies between.

Wendover village neath the hill
Boasts brick and flint traditions still,
For church, clock tower and mill survive
To keep this heritage alive.

Wagons and drays of yesterday
In corners stand and rust away,
Recalling with what toil and tears
Our bread was won in former years.

The log-carts now museumed lie;
No axes ring, no wood chips fly;
Pheasants and flowers gladly share
The woods with walkers passing there.

With *bodgers* and chair-makers gone,
We might lack chairs to sit upon -
But while she still gives life *de luxe*
We'll stand . . . and cheer for *leafy Bucks*!

Henry Pitkin

AN INVITATION TO CROYDON

There's much to see in Croydon Town
A place of interest and renown.
Historic places, an old Airport too
That is well remembered from World War 2.

The Fairfield Halls is the place for you
With such variety the whole year through,
Theatre lovers have the chance
To see a play, or learn to dance.

The Library and the Old Town Hall
Are central, and quite free to all,
Computers, videos, books old and new
Are used by students and older folk too.

The gardens and parks are a joy to behold,
From spring through to autumn when leaves turn to gold:
Coombe Park is the *show-piece* which draws many a crowd,
The gardens are well kept, of this we are proud.

The shopping facilities really are great,
Two traffic-free precincts that keep open late;
The Whitgift and Drummond are Centres of fame
With so many stores that are well known by name.

If you like a place that is near London Town
The trains are quite frequent, and go up and down
To Gatwick or Heathrow, to country or coast,
The connections are excellent, of that we can boast.

The Archbishop's Palace and Whitgift School too
Are historic and famous, and interesting for you:
Croydon has so much of fame and of wealth,
Why not make an excursion, and see for yourself.

Trixie Burnham

AUTUMN BY THE MOLE

The dancing reed of our river Mole
Twinkling in the sunshine
It touches my soul.

Along her banks
Hawthorn berries hang in plenty
Across glistening water a poplar
Upright, as a sentry.

The willow hangs over the river supreme
Their leaves a falling
As sunlight, bounces along their beams

Autumn always looks best in the morning sun
The last of the bees
Well, listen to their hum.

The cascading hips of the wild rose
So stunningly red
They hang in a pose
The squawk of magpies an shrill of the wren
A mallard, so coloured
I'll be back, again and again.

Trevor J Smith

THE OLD READING MUSEUM

Don't go to school today Matthew,
Go to rainy town,
To take some time, to wander round,
The Museum of the odd,
The library of the drunk.

While backs are turned,
Tiptoe across the mosaic of Rome,
To the stuffed stags and badgers,
To the biscuit times of home,
To the unburied Saxon's bones
Pierced by a rusty spear,
To the old fire cart and the
Dusty bottles of beer.

A quick slide down the banisters away
To where, around the walls of oak,
The bouncer librarians stand
And the daytime drunks roam.
Hiding from the greasy rain,
Hiding, until the pubs awaken again.
Bookworms and the drunk
All reading in a dry reading room.

You will remember this, Matthew.
Eccentric, rundown it will leave a mark
And a feeling for our town.

Matthew Farrall

A DAY OUT IN SURREY

Stately homes, some National Trust
Though quite tiring are a must
Should you go down to the Thames at Kew
What pleasure as the river comes in view.

Visit the gardens at Wisley
Acres of botanical beauty
The rock garden with water cascading
Armies of coloured flowers parading

Guildford Cathedral stands proud on a hill
The ponds at Frensham are tranquil and still
Tread the North Downs at your leisure
Visit the Wildlife Trust for good measure

Thorpe Park's the place for a family day out,
Up Loggers Leap; hear the children shout
The Thunder River guarantees a wetting
A lot of fun and laughs. Who's betting
No one will want to leave at the end of the day
Come once to Surrey and you will want to stay.

Elizabeth Miles

THE SILENT POOL

Across the green fields of Surrey,
By the woods, at the foot of the hill
There lies a pool - *The Silent Pool*
Where the waters are still so still.

In the reign of King John, long ago
Came a beautiful girl to the pool
A wood nymph - a woodman's daughter
To bathe in the pool so cool.

Her beauty was famed throughout Surrey
And the demon Prince John came to see
This Naiad whose beauty was legend
A gypsy bathing naked and free.

He resolved to seduce sweet Emma
And charged on his steed through the pool
But Emma surrendered her body
To the depths of her lovely pool.

Her brother Tetbert sought to save her
But the waters called out from the deep
And locked in each other's arms
They sank - into eternal sleep.

The great beeches closed over the water
And silence pervaded the air
Emma's pool had offered her sanctuary
From dishonour too great to bear.

For the lovely children who died here
This crystal pool silently weeps
Where the water is deep and green and clear
And even the kingfisher sleeps.

Beryl Marvin

THE OLD SUTTON OAK

I do wonder what you have seen,
For all these years that you have been,
Sitting, silent, on that spot:
Standing majestic upon your motte,
Watching as the weary world does pass,
Watching through your woody eyeglass.
Watching the wars, the human devastation:
Their race's strides towards self-elimination.
Watching history slowly unfold,
To reveal occurrences prior untold.
Watching the old years pass away,
As slowly the future becomes today.

While ye, oh ancient oak,
Have stood there watching the affairs of folk,
That passed you by, ignoring your wisdom,
That you have acquired watching our little kingdom:
Our horses go, our cars be born,
Historical oaths and vows sworn.
The crusaders leave, the wars fought,
The death, pain and anguish they brought.
You have, most of all these things,
Seen the wrath of our feudal kings;
You have seen Nonsuch Palace built,
And again demolished - without shame or guilt.
You have seen the reformation,
Our revolution, our restoration,
Oh, ancient, wise and learned tree,
In recollection, what can you see,
In your age old memory?

Stephen Bartlet-Jones

A TRIBUTE TO BUCKINGHAMSHIRE

Books have been written on Buckinghamshire,
  Of Kings, and Hampdens, Cromwell, and Squire.
Has anyone thought of Poetry?
  No? Perhaps it is left to you and to me!

What a beautiful County i s Bucks -
  With its fields, and woods, and Aylesbury Ducks.
Woodland scenes of bluebell beds,
  Primrose and cowslips in the hedge.

Footpaths to wander many a mile
  Through winding lane and over stile
The forests of Beech made the furniture trade,
  By Bodgers of old, in the woods chairs were made.

The story of lace should also be told
  Of bobbins with fingers so nimble to hold
To make such patterns as ever was seen
  Fit to adorn our most gracious Queen.

For crackling and clangers we oft did sigh
  - Not pie in the sky, but a pig in the sty
Was our fathers' concern
  As we so often did learn!

Cherry pie suppers at each Harvest Time
  Were just so delicious; to dance and to mime,
To enjoy supper and sing harvest song
  Is a memory from which it does not seem too long.

Alas for our trees, so many have been felled
  And to close my brief story I am surely compelled.
But with its woods, fields, and flowers, I hope you'll agree
  That Buckinghamshire beauty belongs to you and to me.

Margaret L Wright

THE GREAT PLANE TREE OF CARSHALTON

The plane tree has stood for over 200 years in the village of Carshalton, Surrey.
It is one of the largest plane trees in the country.

First the ground was empty and bare
Only rain and sun rays settled there.
When the earth was ready to conceive
The wind blew in a fertile seed,
Covered it with a layer of dust.
Waited, rested and at a time just
As we are born to live and grow
The surface breaks, a birth, for all to know
Life has started with a struggle
And to survive through all the muddle
Of youth's sweet dreams, growing up,
And ages memories, like spilling cup
The storms and calms man made or real
Effect us all, how we grow or feel
So the tree survived, it grew and grew
Over two hundred years into a sky of blue
Now a king amongst plants and trees
Its knowledge of life what it sees
All contained in that ageing bark
Protecting guarding from day to dark
Standing strong, proud and tall
Making us all look so very small
Tree, this tree will live forever,
Man alone must harm it never
For nature gave for all to see
Live on, live long oh mighty tree.

Mike Bloomfield

LITTLE TOWN WITH A BIG HEART

The express to London thundering through
Leaves a strange kind of peace in its wake
Surrounding fields glisten with morning dew
A distant hum heralds another day break

The river, unhurried, gurgles and plays
The workers battling, unlistening, too much to do
Little town waking, we go our separate ways,
Our destiny lies out there, our hearts lie with you

A majestic church spire casts shadows cool and deep
Graceful, timeless houses with a half-timbered frame
A football match, a cricket match, a trophy to keep,
A community that cares, young and old the same

Darkness falls on rain-soaked streets
Lights from the tavern create a neon haze
This little town with a big heart
Holding treasured memories of bygone days.

Lynne Russell

GUILDFORD IN SURREY

Have you been to Guildford in Surrey?
It's a town you can miss if you hurry
From Portsmouth to London going by train
Not breaking your journey, just straight home again
Missing North Street to High Street via Swan Lane
You could overlook Guildford in Surrey

There's history at Guildford in Surrey
Town Guides show you round without hurry
Churches, a Castle, and old buildings too
A Town Clock familiar to many of you
The High Street to climb for a very fine view
Of the Hogs Back near Guildford in Surrey

The Wey runs through Guildford in Surrey
But if you can't row do not worry
Booking a seat on a boat can be done
In summer months a boat trip is fun
If you easily burn beware of the sun
When cruising Guildford's Wey in Surrey

Flowers bloom all round Guildford in Surrey
Though keeping costs within budget's a worry
The gardeners work hard planting masses of flowers
The outcome gives pleasure for numerous hours
So while sitting quietly in one of the bowers
Admire Guildford's beauty in Surrey

So come to Guildford in Surrey
Take time for your visit, don't hurry
There's much to see, to hear and do
Enjoy a swim or skating too
At Spectrum it's the place for you
It all happens at Guildford in Surrey

Yvonne V Smith

FICTION LIBRARY

(Thoughts while browsing in the Fiction Section, Sutton Library, Sutton)

A world of words, oppressive in their weight
Like seething crowds, remote and desolate.
But each has its own character and voice
To be released and quickened by a choice.

The teeming titles span the utmost range
From passionate and trad to weird and strange,
The content - from opinion clear and sound -
Is everything from trivial to profound.

We need this world as we need earth and home,
A million minds to it for succour turn.
What else provides - exclude TV and tape -
Such instant pleasure, interest and escape?

Anew, brought into being year by year,
The world of books, perpetual, will appear.
From out the writers' laboured mind it grows -
Into an aching human deep it goes.

Adamson Brown

INFORMATION

We hope you have enjoyed reading this book - and that you will continue to enjoy it in the coming years.

If you like reading and writing poetry drop us a line, or give us a call, and we'll send you a free information pack.

Write to

Arrival Press Information
1-2 Wainman Road
Woodston
Peterborough
PE2 7BU.